THINKING ABOUT
OUR KIDS

THINKING ABOUT OUR KIDS

HAROLD HOWE II

THE FREE PRESS
A Division of Macmillan, Inc.
NEW YORK

Maxwell Macmillan Canada
TORONTO

Maxwell Macmillan International
NEW YORK   OXFORD   SINGAPORE   SYDNEY

The Free Press
A Division of Macmillan, Inc.
866 Third Avenue, New York, N.Y. 10022

Maxwell Macmillan Canada, Inc.
1200 Eglinton Avenue East
Suite 200
Don Mills, Ontario M3C 3N1

Macmillan, Inc. is part of the Maxwell Communication Group of Companies

Printed in the United States of America

printing number

1   2   3   4   5   6   7   8   9   10

Library of Congress Cataloging-in-Publication Data
Howe, Harold
   Thinking about our kids / Harold Howe II.
      p.   cm
   Includes bibliographical references (p.   ) and index.
   ISBN 0-02-915294-1
      1. Educational change—United States. 2. School management and organization—
   United States. 3. Education—United States—Aims and objectives. 4. Education—
   Social aspects—United States.
   I. Title.
   LA217.2.H69   1993
   370'.973—dc20   93–25789
                                                                        CIP

"School Choice," editorial, *The Boston Globe*, February, 13, 1991. Reprinted courtesy of *The Bloston Globe*.

Harold Howe II, "We Need Four More National Education Goals," *Education Week*, XII: 19, February 3, 1993, pp. 44, 32. Reprinted with permission from *Education Week*.

CONTENTS

PREFACE

This book emerges more from experience than from scholarship. I have been an active educator for fifty-two years, with about four years off for military service in World War II. And come to think of it I would classify those years in the Navy as representing continuity in the realm of education. Most of them were spent trying to teach the crew of a minesweeper how to avoid blowing themselves up or how to chase submarines or how to deal with catastrophes at sea. All of these skills I presumably had been taught a few months earlier at the Naval Mine Warfare School in Yorktown, Virginia. Like most new school teachers, I had learned the theory and not the practice and therefore dealt with reality the hard way, by making mistakes and correcting them. Fortunately, my mistakes did not prove fatal.

After many years of muddling about in schools, colleges, and the public and private agencies that serve them, I am still persuaded that the best way to learn about something is to do it. In fact, one of my strongest convictions about improving education is that we need to make better use of the power of experience in the learning process. There is no better way to learn something about politics than by working in a campaign. And if that's not possible, there are ways to simulate that experience that are more powerful than reading a textbook.

My years in education have included work in private schools as a history teacher and in public schools as a school principal and superintendent, in North Carolina as a change-agent for education governor Terry Sanford, in Washington as President Johnson's chief education officer, and in the Ford Foundation with responsibility for philanthropic initiatives in both higher education and schools in the United States and India. These endeavors have enriched my thinking about the ramifications of educational practice, problems, and policies.

Other realms of experience, too, lie behind what this book has to say. One is personal. My family and particularly my father filled my early years with exposures to education that went beyond my own attendance at school and college. He was a Presbyterian minister, an All-American quarterback, a private school teacher, chaplain, administrator, and coach, a conscientious objector in World War I, a college professor at Dartmouth, and for twelve years the president of a predominantly black private college in Virginia, Hampton Institute (now Hampton University).

This institution was founded in the mid-1860s by my maternal grandfather, a son of missionaries to Hawaii and the commander of a black regiment in the Civil War. He launched Hampton Institute while working for the Freedmen's Bureau, the federal agency created to assist blacks with the transition from slavery to freedom. During my secondary school and college years, my family lived at Hampton—then an island of desegregated faculty and black students in a totally segregated society. This combi-

nation of forebears with a strong element of social con-
science and exposure to life in the South before the *Brown*
decision no doubt helped to shape my views about education and society.

Another realm of experience has been a rich mix of
extracurricular activities related to my broad interest in
education. There have been so many of these that a listing
would be boring, so I will mention just one of them: from
1988 to 1992, I chaired the William T. Grant Foundation's
activity called Youth and America's Future: The William T.
Grant Foundation Commission on Work, Family, and
Citizenship. The Commission issued a report entitled *The
Forgotten Half*, about which I will have more to say later in
this book. My work with the Commission brought about a
major change in my thinking about education. It taught me
that the learning young people acquire in families, communities, and a variety of other settings is as important a part
of their education as the learning that takes place in school.

Finally, the last eleven years have given me new and
mind-opening experiences as a member of the faculty at
the Harvard Graduate School of Education. This opportunity appeared by chance. I met the late Paul Ylvisaker, who
was then the Dean of Education at Harvard, on a railroad
train in 1980. He asked me what I was planning to do after
retiring from the Ford Foundation, and he suggested I join
the Harvard faculty—an idea that had never occurred to
me. I had seen myself as a practitioner of and advocate for
education rather than as a person who studied it, wrote
about it, and taught it as a professional field of learning. I
was at home in the governance of universities through my
roles as trustee and foundation officer, but the professors I

thought of as beings in a rarefied atmosphere, where it might be hard for me to breathe.

In spite of these worries about fitting into academia, I took the plunge in the academic year 1981-82. After eleven years of floundering around Harvard, I now think that, next to my luck in matrimony some fifty-three years ago, this has been the best experience of my life. Beyond the obvious appeal of Harvard as a fine place for a Yale man to spend his declining years, it has brought me into contact with a wonderful group of faculty members and students, and I have learned from both. My thinking about educational matters has been broadened and deepened by this experience.

I am indebted to many people for assisting me with this book. My wife, Sibby, has patiently listened to my reading of drafts and made suggestions for clarity. Aaron Fink, a long-time colleague in educational affairs, has been generous with time and cogent advice. Samuel Halperin, director of the William T. Grant Foundation Commission on Work, Family, and Citizenship, has also contributed to my thinking on these matters. Patricia Graham has been a patient and stimulating colleague since 1982, when she became Harvard's first female dean. Eric von Zinkernagel managed to collect all the articles, essays, and speeches I have produced over the years and put together a bibliography. His work helped me to look back and discover the changes in my own thinking during fifty-two years of experience in education.

Others who have helped me are Paul Barton, John Collins, Nancy Cole, Joan First, Jay Heubert, George Madaus, Kim Marshall, Katherine Merseth, Terry Saario,

PREFACE

and F. Champion Ward. Theodore Sizer and James Comer reviewed my observations about their activities. Special thanks go to Donna Schroth, whose help with digging up information, preparing drafts, and keeping my affairs in order while the book was in process have made the project possible. Arthur Rosenthal talked me into writing the book. It took him about three years to pin me down, but he kept at it and persuaded me that it was worth doing. He also helped me to get invaluable editorial assistance from Camille Smith, a master of the art of writing succinctly.

I am grateful to the William T. Grant Foundation and the Spencer Foundation for helping with these endeavors, as well as to the Rockefeller Foundation, which invited Samuel Halperin and me along with our spouses to its Bellagio Study and Conference Center on Lake Como in northern Italy to work together for five weeks.

This book is full of opinions. None of the above people should be held responsible for them. Indeed some of them urged me to change them. Both these opinions and any errors of fact are all mine.

THINKING ABOUT
OUR KIDS

Introduction:
Reforming the Reformers

Those of us who are interested in improving education have a habit of paying too much attention to schools and not enough to children. American education is standing in the need of prayer, but not entirely for the reasons typically proposed by the prophets of the so-called school reform movement. Much of that movement today is based on an erroneous assumption—that we can fix the schools so that the schools can fix the kids. This assumption ignores the large part of children's lives that takes place outside of school. Education happens around the clock, in the family and the community as well as in school. Families and communities, depending on their circumstances, can be educators in their own right as well as powerful agents for reinforcing what is taught in school, enhancing learning, and fostering the development of maturity and responsibility—or they can be the opposite. Accordingly, I see the reform of education in our country as a much broader issue than the improvement of schooling.

This broader understanding of education is largely missing from the major government-sponsored publications on educational reform of the past decade. There have been three such documents: *A Nation at Risk: The Imperative for Educational Reform*, issued by the National Commission on Excellence in Education in 1983; the *National Education Goals*, issued by the governors and the President in 1989; and *America 2000: An Education Strategy*, issued by the President and the Secretary of Education in 1991. These three documents now strongly influence a high percentage of action in our country on *school reform* and a relatively small proportion of action on *educational reform*. I will have more to say about their shortcomings later on.

Four major themes, all of them neglected in these documents, dominate the argument in this book. Each concerns changes that I believe are essential if we are to create a system of education that will serve the needs of all our children and our nation.

First, as I have said, it is time to stop thinking of education as what happens in school. It is time to recognize the educational role of families, communities, and other social institutions outside the schools. We need a commitment from government and private agencies to pursue this broad definition of education as vigorously as they pursue school improvement. This commitment must include the recognition that factors not usually considered directly relevant to education, such as poverty and racial discrimination, in fact have a strong impact on learning in general and on success in school.

Second, within the schools, I believe we must make major changes in what happens in classrooms. To do this we must revise the factory model of schooling that is so well established in the United States. That model, with its classroom routines designed to turn students into assembly-line products, must give way to classroom routines that make classrooms exciting places to be and in which students take much more active roles than they typically do today.

Third, we must recognize that the population of the United States and of the schools is becoming increasingly diverse. It is vital today and will be even more so tomorrow that we learn to build understanding and respect among the races and cultures that make up this nation. Educational institutions must foster such understanding and respect in ways that enrich our social diversity rather than tangle it in rivalries and abrasions.

Finally, political and educational leaders in school districts, states, and national government must be attentive to the fiscal needs of schools. We need a new system of financing elementary and secondary education based on the educational needs of children and on fairness to all economic and social groups as well as fairness to taxpayers. It is time to address the simple fact that today a child's chance for a decent school is controlled by where the child happens to live.

These important themes, as I said, were either not mentioned at all or given very limited attention in the three major national documents on educational reform. For example, *America 2000*, which outlined the educational strategy of the Bush administration, created a concept of four trains on four separate tracks rushing toward the year 2000. Here are some highlights of what was to be on each track:

Track I: A "15-point accountability package," with the focus on measuring achievement and rewarding it. "World class standards" and new tests called American Achievement Tests in five core subjects. Citations and scholarships to reward students who do well on the tests. Report cards to show how students, schools, districts, and states are doing. Encouragement of school choice policies and school-level decisionmaking. Monetary awards for schools that make notable progress. Academies to train school leaders and teachers. Differential pay and alternative paths to certification for teachers. Awards for outstanding teachers.

Track II: A "New Generation of American Schools," beginning with 535 such schools created with "limited federal support for start-up costs."* Encouragement of communities to become "America 2000 Communities" by adopting the National Education Goals, developing strategies to achieve them, designing report cards to measure results, and supporting New American Schools.

Track III: An emphasis on adult literacy and on upgrading the skills of those already in the labor force.

Track IV: A challenge to every town in America to become an America 2000 Community as defined in Track II.

---

*In fact only eleven such schools have been set up, and there is considerable doubt today about their chances of survival.

INTRODUCTION: REFORMING THE REFORMERS

Nowhere on any of these tracks do we find recognition of the educational importance of children's lives (and living conditions) outside the school, of the need to replace factory schools with more humane and exciting environments for learning, or of the responsibility of the schools to come to terms in constructive ways with America's increasing diversity.

In the spring of 1992 a large section of the city of Los Angeles was destroyed and some thirty Americans were wantonly killed. Twenty-five years earlier similar outbreaks had ravaged the same section of Los Angeles and parts of numerous other cities as well. A major study of those earlier events called for attention to the unmet needs of the poor in America's central cities and to the pervasiveness of racial discrimination in our society. During the ensuing quarter-century repeated calls for racial and economic fairness went unheard by those in power.

It is painfully unsurprising to me that Los Angeles blew up again. It, like other U.S. cities, had been shouting for help for a quarter of a century and had received none—not from Jimmy Carter, a Democrat; not from Ronald Reagan, a Californian; not from George Bush, a self-appointed Education President. On the contrary, over those years the contribution of federal resources to American cities steadily eroded. At present we are failing to educate all our citizens about one another, and we are failing to provide our growing number of poverty-stricken children with decent living conditions. Our failure to respond to the cities' call for help creates a time bomb waiting to destroy civility in urban America.

From the absence of such concerns in the documents on

educational reform, it seems that those who issued the documents saw the issue of making a diverse society work as having nothing to do with education. How naive could they be? It has everything to do with education! Do they really believe that hunger, homelessness, lack of health care, and other manifestations of poverty and discrimination have nothing to do with success in school? Do they really believe that our schools need pay no attention to interracial and intercultural feelings in American society? If so, these are not the only issues on which these doctors of America's educational illness could use a dose of clear thinking. In addition to these flagrant omissions, their prescriptions are marked by a number of other serious misunderstandings about what needs curing in American education and what the treatment should be.

One such misunderstanding is that the goals of American schools should be dictated by political figures. Another is that the best way to improve schools is by imposing new tests and standards from the top down. Then there is the cherished misapprehension that average scores on standardized tests are a reliable guide to the quality of our schools; related to this is the belief that the best way to motivate children and teachers is to use test scores to exhibit their failures, thus encouraging them to work hard to get better test scores. Still another dubious notion is that the main purpose of schooling is to rescue the country's corporations from their problems of international competition; its corollary is the view that our current economic slowdown is mainly attributable to the weaknesses of schools. Although the growing cooperation of the business community with education has had some very useful effects, this linking of schools and business is part of what is behind the naive belief that instituting a system of school choice, with competition as its guiding principle, will be a panacea for whatever ails the schools.

These questionable beliefs and practices will come in for further scrutiny in later chapters, as will the more positive side of what is happening in American education. Within schools and in other realms with powerful educational influence on children and youth, both new ideas and old, well-tested practices hold promise for improving learning. Factory-model schools are being replaced in some districts by new concepts of schooling that make students active participants in their own learning. Multicultural education and other initiatives are encouraging students to reach across the barriers of race and culture and learn to understand one another. These and other steps already being taken serve as examples of what can be accomplished once we discard the misunderstandings about both what ails the schools and what will cure them.

In my experience with schools since I first taught in 1940, I can't remember a time when the education community faced a more complex and more significant set of choices about the guts of its business. There was a major flurry in the late 1950s when the Soviets sent up a satellite before we did, awakening a rash of self-criticism about science and mathematics in American schools. But the stakes involved in today's controversies are wider and deeper in their implications for American society than were those occasioned by Sputnik. As we approach the twenty-first

THINKING ABOUT OUR KIDS

century in a society characterized by an ever-richer variety of cultural backgrounds and an ever-widening economic gap between the well-off and the poor, we must change the very definition of education to include the world beyond the schoolhouse door.

1

Misuse of Tests to
Measure Schools

Tests have become the tail that wags the dog in the public discussion of educational change in the United States. Since the publication of *A Nation at Risk*, in which the National Commission on Excellence in Education announced that "The College Board's Scholastic Aptitude Tests (SAT) demonstrate a virtually unbroken decline from 1963 to 1980,"[1] there has been a panicky feeling that falling average scores on standardized tests show that our schools are not educating students as well as they used to. The widely held notion that schools have gone downhill since the good old days when average SAT scores were higher is what brought on the so-called school reform movement of the late seventies and early eighties.

When concern about this imagined decline in the quality of our schools was combined with declarations from business that it was unable to compete in the world market because American workers were undereducated, political leaders jumped on the school-improvement bandwagon. The public impression that taxes spent on schools were yielding a negative return added to the political heat that produced a firestorm of what Arthur Wise has called "legislated learning," most of it brought on by governors and state legislatures but some of it emerging from other sources. Literally hundreds of local, state, and national studies in the 1980s started with the same rhetoric: Test scores show that our schools are teaching less effectively than in the past; poorly educated workers are undermining our competitive edge overseas and destroying our prosperity; these trends must be reversed by fundamental changes in our schools.

The logic behind this rhetoric is seriously flawed. For one thing, I believe that the connection between lower test scores and declining economic competitiveness has been considerably exaggerated. Many factors other than the supposed decline in the quality of schools are influencing the productivity of our workers. I will have more to say about the dependence of American business on schooling in Chapter 9. In the meantime, a quotation from Clark Kerr, a noted labor economist and educator, will suffice to undergird my contention that the erosion of American productivity can be traced to many causes outside the schools.

> If not education almost alone (as is generally claimed), then who did it? Everybody. ... We spent too much and saved too little and invested too little. We spent too little of our research and development funds on industrial improvement and too much on the military. We turned too much to easy self-gratification, as in drugs, alcohol, and crime, and TV for

the children instead of homework. ... We put too much emphasis on advertising and too little on quality in production. We paid too little attention to human relations in industry—Japanese-managed firms in America achieve Japanese levels of quantity and quality from American workers.[2]

Not only is it an oversimplification to blame declining productivity on the schools; I also believe that a very large proportion of recent rhetoric about test scores proving that our schools have gone downhill is just plain hokum. Let's take a closer look at the major sources of information purported to demonstrate this American educational disaster: the "decline" in SAT scores and America's presumed low standing on the scoreboard of international tests.

Declining SAT Scores

Why did average SAT scores fall rapidly in the years 1963–1975, and why have they remained at lower levels while jiggling up and down since then? There are two main points to be made in response to this query. The first is that no one can fully explain all the changes in SAT scores over the years. Numerous possible explanations have been proposed, including one that attaches variation in average scores to the proportion of first-born children taking the test—an idea that I find a bit of a stretch. The second, and much more important, point is that changes in the economic and social backgrounds of students taking the test account for a very large proportion of the change in scores. In earlier years, when fewer high school students went on to college, candidates who took the SAT tended to be those who had been most successful in high school and/or were from relatively privileged backgrounds. When college doors opened more widely and colleges that had not used the SAT before began to do so, a larger proportion of students from deprived backgrounds, and often from second-rate schools, aspired to college and therefore started to take the tests. The result was a reduction in average test scores because of those students' deprivations and inadequate educational preparation, not because of any erosion of the quality of schools.

The College Board appointed a "blue-ribbon panel" (of which I was vice chairman) to determine the reasons for the falling SAT scores. The panel found in 1977 that two-thirds of the decline in average scores between 1963 and 1971 was attributable to the fact that new and different students were taking the test.[3] My own sense is that even more than two-thirds of the decline came about because more poor and minority students were aspiring to college. The growth of federal and state programs to enable such students to attend college was encouraging their aspirations. So it is quite clear that the falling SAT scores were in large part a signal of hope and promise, not an indicator of school failure. Of course, many of these new candidates for admission to college, often the first in their families to apply, scored lower than average on the SAT. Both their schools and their family and community supports for school success were often inferior to those of middle-class students. In a way, then, the lower SAT scores were good news: they signaled a major gain in equality of educational opportunity.

MISUSE OF TESTS TO MEASURE SCHOOLS

In 1984, in an article entitled "Let's Have Another SAT Score Decline,"[4] I argued the case for getting a still larger proportion of high school graduates to go to college, even though it would lower the average test scores further. I still believe this is a good idea. A major theme of American education in the last two centuries has been the slow but steady extension of the opportunity for higher education to people from all economic classes and all social and cultural groups—just the opposite of the basic assumption in many European countries until quite recently. The years since 1960 have seen steady increases in college attendance by Americans from disadvantaged backgrounds. The fact that this change brings lower average test scores is unimportant. But an immense amount of significance has been assigned to it because it is mistakenly seen as a signal of declining quality in the schools. In America, things are supposed to get better, and when they don't, someone has to be blamed.

Average SAT scores are not a valid basis for comparing schools or school districts or states with one another, not only because different proportions of students with varied backgrounds take the test but also because the average test scores of any group are powerfully influenced by the personal circumstances of test takers. The idea that such tests measure only the outcomes of schooling is, to put it bluntly, pure baloney. Indeed, the College Board says in its explanation of the SAT that it measures all the test taker's learning experience, both in and out of school. A person's scores are influenced by many factors in the home, such as parents' reading habits, availability of books and magazines, associations with peers and parents that involve the discussion of ideas, family expectations about homework, a quiet place to study, and the good fortune of having stimulating experiences in the family's leisure time. Many children of poverty, a rapidly growing group in America, get short-changed in these realms of learning outside of school. In addition, all too frequently their schools are underfunded, overcrowded, and ill-prepared to provide the special help they require if they are to succeed with learning. Homeless and migrant children get doubly shortchanged. And all of these conditions affect SAT scores.

Commenting on the tendency of Americans to see test scores as the only measure of school quality rather than as what they actually are, "a fallible indicator of a small slice of what schools do," George Madaus of the Center for the Study of Testing, Evaluation, and Educational Policy at Boston College has this to say:

> I believe that the use of tests as *the* measure of schooling grows out of the factory metaphor for schools, that considers the student a product that can talk or a commodity to be shaped. The test becomes the quality control criterion at the expense of all other ends. The means to measure ends become the ends in themselves.
>
> Further, until other concomitant reforms are put in place—health, social support systems, family, and educational resources—any measure of achievement will be neither a good measure nor a just measure.[5]

Misunderstandings about the meaning of average SAT scores have plagued our thinking about educational issues ever since such averages began to be published annually. An admirer and supporter of the College Board and a participant in some of its affairs, I now think it could have handled these misunderstandings more effectively. It is a great temptation to the College Board to act as if it is responsible for the yardstick for measuring American schooling. It might rethink its pontifical annual announcements of a two-point increase in math scores or a three-point decline in verbal scores with attendant remarks about progress or gloom in the prospects of schools. The true significance of these events is about the same as a ten- or fifteen-point change in the Dow Jones index of stocks.

Another reason the SAT is not a measure of the quality or performance of schools is that most students in school don't take it. But even if they did it would not be an adequate measure of schooling alone. In spite of these facts, the decline in SAT scores has been powerfully and frequently presented as evidence of the deterioration of American schools and the need for changes in them. Schools do need to change, but not because of average SAT scores.

As an example of the misleading equation of test scores and school quality, consider New Hampshire, a state with some good schools and some bad ones, but one that has been at or near the top in average SAT scores. There are many school districts in New Hampshire that provide a second- or third-rate education for their students because the schools are starved for adequate funding. Of all the fifty states, New Hampshire provides the least state tax funding for schools, thus leaving children almost completely at the mercy of local school district resources. It is the only state that still does not require kindergarten for five-year-olds. This matter is left to local option, and some of the state's school boards save money for their taxpayers by denying a good start in learning to little children who can't vote. It would make more educational sense to omit the senior year of high school!

I found another, less troubling example of misuse of average SAT scores several years ago when Eastern Airlines was still alive. Its magazine carried an advertisement paid for by the state of Oklahoma urging businesses to consider locating there because the state's average SAT scores were quite high. Very few students in Oklahoma take the SAT—mostly those who want to leave the state to attend colleges that require it. If around fifty percent of Oklahoma students took the SAT, as they do in some other states, Oklahoma's average score would be much lower. Corporations that built new plants in Oklahoma to take advantage of its workforce with high levels of learning no doubt got a surprise.

Early in the 1980s, when Ted Bell was Secretary of Education in Washington, he invented his famous Wall Chart, which displayed the average SAT scores of all states. This massive supply of comparative misinformation sparked a hue and cry. Gregory Anrig, the president of the Educational Testing Service, wrote Secretary Bell annually to suggest that he cease publishing materials that confused the public. But Bell continued issuing the Wall Chart and included with it information about the percentage of test takers behind each state's average, along with other interpretive material about poverty and racial or cultural groups. With these added data it was possible, if you were a well-trained quantitative social scientist, to recompute the pecking order of states on the chart. Such an exercise would move New Hampshire—and Oklahoma—much further down the rank order of states. But the general public never hears about this confusing situation or doesn't understand it.

Much more could be said about the SAT. It is the best test of its kind. When its scores are properly used it is relatively free of racial or cultural bias, even though counterclaims on this point are numerous. When used for the purpose for which it is intended, helping colleges and students consider each other sensibly, it makes a positive contribution to the transition from school to college. Its multiple-choice questions do not simply ask students to recall facts, as is often charged; many of its test items, on the contrary, require advanced and complex thinking. One of its advantages over other tests now being considered is its low cost per student. It has a major advantage that some see as a disadvantage, namely, that it has little or no impact on what is taught in schools or how it is taught, thus leaving schools to consider their curriculum free from outside intrusion—a condition sometimes called academic freedom. But it is not and does not pretend to be a useful instrument for judging schools or state systems of education. Neither should it be used, as it sometimes is, to decide who can play football.

Another test very much like the SAT is the PSAT—the Preliminary Scholastic Aptitude Test, which is usually offered for guidance purposes a year or two earlier than the SAT. It takes less time, costs less, and produces a score that predicts quite well the performance of a student on the more comprehensive SAT. I mention the PSAT here because useful recent data on it are conveniently available: studies of the performance of *carefully matched groups of students*. In four comparisons over the years 1960-1983, the groups of students from similar backgrounds had average scores that were almost identical. In other words, when the differing backgrounds of the test takers were removed from the picture, PSAT test takers over the years of the so-called decline in SAT scores showed no decline in their average scores.

This information strongly supports my view that the change in SAT scores, in all likelihood, has been even more strongly influenced by the expansion of the pool of test takers than was suggested by the College Board's blue-ribbon panel.

A Nation at Risk, while citing declining SAT scores as a major piece of evidence of the failure of America's schools, did not discuss the PSAT averages. And there was some hesitancy about dealing with them in the 1977 report of the blue-ribbon panel: "An accounting of the complex variety of factors that emerged in the panel's examination of this difference between the SAT and PSAT/MSQT patterns would burden this report unduly." The fact is that the data on PSAT test scores cast a shadow on the usual explanations for the falling SAT scores. If the views of the National Commission on Excellence in Education were applied to these PSAT results, then instead of using SAT scores to "prove" the sorry state of American schools, the Commission would have to turn 180 degrees and congratulate the schools for the consistency of their performance.

I am quite aware that some of these reflections about interpreting test scores are problematical, but that is another point I am trying to make. In our enthusiasm for testing as the sole measurement of schooling, we have managed to create a new academic industry based on arguing about the meaning of test scores. It is a highly technical enterprise. Many ordinary educators are repelled by its complexity. There are responsible and able people engaged in it, and there are others whose contributions are driven by ideology rather than objective analysis. The result is that the messages received by the public are frequently without merit. One of the real needs to keep in mind in our future thinking about schools is the need for intermediaries who understand psychometricians and can translate their ideas for the rest of us.

Just a simple example to document this viewpoint: well-meaning journalists and business leaders engaged with educators frequently assert that all students in the fourth grade should be reading at the fourth-grade level as measured by standardized tests. They don't understand that such a view is somewhat analogous to requiring all the football teams in the country to win more than half their games. When certain reading scores are taken as the norm for reading "at a fourth-grade level," fourth graders will always include readers above and below that standard. And if those below rise to the norm, the norm for fourth graders will soon be raised. When our business friends and political leaders can grasp such matters, they will be as helpful as they would like to be. In the meantime, test developers and users have an obligation to explain their mumbo-jumbo more clearly than they typically do.

There is no limit to the imaginations of people seeking explanations for the decline in SAT scores. When a College Board researcher discovered that the growth and spread of the score decline paralleled the growth and spread of McDonald's restaurants, I wrote what was supposed to be an amusing piece on how imbibing junk food had reduced the test-taking capacity of youth by bringing them to the test in a soporific state. But some people took it seriously, particularly the part of it in which I argued that a recent small increase in test scores was caused by the introduction of the McDonald's fish sandwich (fish having long been known as brain food). The blue-ribbon panel's report mentions some additional gems for those interested in this elusive topic to consider:

> Still others attribute the decline to a "growing rejection of traditional religions" and to a concomitant turning to "religions of the East, drug-related religions, mysticism, witchcraft, astrology," or with different emphasis, to a growing "preference for fantasy over reality" and "celebration of the ideology of irrationalism," in which knowledge is attained through intuition, inspiration and revelation.[6]

With all of these possibilities to choose from, one can't help wondering how those who wrote *A Nation at Risk* and so many others after them became so single-mindedly certain that the decline in test scores should be blamed solely on changes in the schools. Today, of course, there is a new counter-explanation of the decline. It argues that there never was a real decline in scores and that the appearance of a decline has been caused by changes in the test-taking group.[7] As I have said, I agree with this view, at least in my belief that the importance of the so-called decline in SAT scores as an indicator of school quality has been heavily exaggerated.

International Test Comparisons

SAT scores are not the only test results that are widely misinterpreted as evidence of the sorry state of American schools. In addition to citing the decline in SAT scores, *A Nation at Risk* included, at the top of its list of "Indicators of the Risk," the following statement: "International comparisons of student achievement completed a decade ago reveal that on 19 academic tests American students were never first or second and, in comparison with other industrialized nations, were last seven times."[8] Like the reference to declining SAT scores, this alarmist announcement found a receptive audience. Many people now express the opinion that American schools are among the worst in the developed world.

This opinion, to the extent that it is based on evidence at all, rests on careless interpretation of data from an international testing program that reaches back to the 1960s. This program, operated by responsible scholars in the United States, Sweden, the United Kingdom, and numerous other countries, provides testing in the major fields of learning and learning skills. It endeavors to test similar samples of students in each country's schools, so that test results will be comparable.

Considering the complexity of the task of developing and administering tests in systems of education that differ in many respects, this program has been carefully planned and increasingly well operated. My complaints are not so much about what it does as about what it doesn't do. I have two concerns that should be given much more attention by those who are responsible for reporting on the results of these tests.

First, they have failed to state directly and clearly the real difficulty of obtaining comparable samples of students in various countries so that test results could be meaningful as international comparisons. Second, and far more important, they have overemphasized the role of schools in producing the test results and underemphasized the contributions of social and cultural factors. Such factors are probably more significant than schools in determining the comparative standings of different countries, but this is seldom pointed out in the publicity about the tests.

Iris Rotberg of the National Science Foundation has done some trenchant writing on the problems of getting valid samples of students for tests that will be used for international comparisons.[9] She points out that the tests given in the 1960s and early 1970s made extensive use of noncomparable samples. This variation in test takers from country to country made the United States come off badly in the comparisons because a high proportion of its young people were enrolled in upper secondary schools. In most European countries only a small percentage of teenagers attended such schools. So, for example, a test of a sample of students in the last year of secondary school would include students from the top nine percent of students in Germany and about the top seventy percent in the United States. If the scores of the top nine percent of U.S. students had been compared with the German scores a very different picture would have emerged.

In an effort to reduce the sampling problem and to get information about knowledge of mathematics and science, the students tested in the twelfth grade were limited to those on the academic track who were taking mathematics and science courses. Apparently it was believed that this would provide more valid comparisons of average scores. But what emerged was a substantial difference between schools depending on whether mathematics was required or optional in grade twelve. Average scores were much higher for students in schools where it was optional. Obviously, the students who performed best on the test were those who had done well in math in earlier grades and had chosen to stay with it; low performers had dropped out of math in schools that allowed them to do so. Although the highest average scores were recorded in schools where mathematics was not required in the twelfth grade, the highest levels of literacy in mathematics were in the lower-scoring schools where it was required. For a true comparison of knowledge of math among all students, the students not taking mathematics should have been included in the tests; their low scores would have reversed the averages of the two groups. The point of wading through this example is that average test scores can have a variety of meanings depending on who takes the test and whose scores are averaged into the equation. And the question of who takes the test is subject to many pressures—some of them political, some educational, and some probably financial.

Many other issues also should be considered in attempts to make valid international comparisons. Social and economic differences in testing samples are major factors affecting test results. Arrangements for administering tests, too, can affect test results. As Rotberg says, "Countries are likely to differ in the criteria they set for excluding regions, schools, students within schools, or even various ethnic and language groups" from the test.[10]

The people who work on preparing and administering international tests are aware of all these difficulties. Often, in their reports on the tests, they do mention factors that might distort international comparisons of scores, but they tend to do so in footnotes that are more understandable to psychometricians than to most educators and that almost never get the attention of the public. What makes the headlines and what has undermined the confidence of Americans in their schools is the pecking-order list of countries showing comparative test scores without adequate direct explanation to qualify their meaning. Headline writers seem to see test scores as analogous to basketball scores: if a team loses three starting players because of injuries, there is no reason to reinterpret the results of the game. Although the tests do offer some useful information about educational practices around the world, the way their results are usually interpreted amounts to an international replica of Ted Bell's Wall Chart—and they are about as accurate as that chart in measuring the quality of schools.

One of the national educational goals issued by the governors and George Bush in 1989 is to make U.S. students first in the world in mathematics and science by the year 2000. As Rotberg points out, information from test scores is not an adequate indicator of America's international standing and may distract us from more important concerns:

> The public perception that the U.S. is falling behind in science and mathematics, embodied in the fourth national goal for education, is based on a narrow criterion that has serious methodological deficiencies. The risk is not simply that we will underestimate our accomplishments. Of far greater importance is the likelihood that too narrow a definition of the problem may lead us to "solutions" that are at best trivial and may indeed be counterproductive to addressing more important problems.[11]

MISUSE OF TESTS TO MEASURE SCHOOLS

One of the countries that generally scores higher than the United States on the international tests is Japan, the country that is mentioned most often in discussions of the U.S. need to have a better-educated workforce so as to be competitive in the world economy. Japan's higher scores on international tests are monotonously interpreted as clear evidence that our schools are at fault. In order to produce a generation of children who can compete with the Japanese, the refrain goes, we must fix our schools. The fact is that comparisons of Japanese and American students based on standardized tests in mathematics and science or in any other fields of learning will not be favorable to the United States in the year 2000 or at any other time in the foreseeable future because of differences between Japanese society and American society that go far beyond schooling.

Simplistic thinking about such comparisons gives little or no attention to significant differences between the two countries that schools cannot control. Japan has had no immigration for thousands of years and maintains a homogeneous society and culture and a single language tradition, while the United States is a nation of immigrants with varied language backgrounds and a recent major influx of people from around the world. The United States has large and growing minority groups who have suffered from slavery, conquest, discrimination, and neglect and are not yet free of all the effects of those burdens; Japan has only a small group of "second-class citizens" because of long-ago caste-like differentiation of workers in certain low-level jobs. The number of American children living in poverty has grown rapidly in recent years; there has been no such development in Japan, and its safety nets for aiding its smaller poor population are much more comprehensive than ours. Furthermore, the American family has undergone major changes since World War II, changes that have undermined many of the family-based supports for children and youth that foster learning, while the Japanese family, though perhaps experiencing pressure to change, remains a powerful motivator and supporter of learning. In Chapter 2 I will have more to say about the effects on U.S. children of the conditions outlined here. For now, it is sufficient to suggest that our school reform movement has underplayed the effects on school performance and test results of broad social issues outside the schools.

Besides keeping in mind these broader factors, we should remember not to take comparisons of test scores at face value. An issue that enters into the comparison of different countries' scores is whether the students being compared have studied a similar curriculum. If they have, then the value of the comparison is enhanced. In the most recent comparison in mathematics for the United States and Japan, the evidence is that American students who had studied a curriculum similar to that of Japanese students did almost as well as the Japanese in both eighth-grade algebra and twelfth-grade calculus. But, not surprisingly, Americans who had not taken these subjects at the time of the test did much worse, pulling down the average score of all American students. Ignoring such subtleties, the 1992 Budget Document of the U.S. Government summarized the results of this study as follows: "U.S. students performed poorly in every grade and in every aspect of mathematics tested."[12]

A decade ago *A Nation at Risk* cited test results, both

domestic and international, as evidence of the decline of our educational system without mentioning the problems of comparing dissimilar groups of students and without considering differing cultural and social factors in the countries involved. Both of these omissions are still all too prevalent today. The risk referred to in the publication's title was not the risk to children's lives and children's learning created by poverty or other difficult circumstances. Instead, it was the risk to the nation's competitive economic position presumably created by our rapidly declining schools.

The next chapter will address some of the social and cultural issues as they relate to the schools and the education of children and youth. But first I want to correct an impression that may by this time have arisen in some readers' minds: "This guy is just a social reformer, not an educator. He thinks the schools are fine." On the contrary, I believe we do need major changes in our schools, and some useful pointers toward these changes are beginning to appear. They are very different from the prescriptions of *A Nation at Risk*, an advocacy effort that has run out of steam partly because it misused testing information as the base for its imperatives. The people who work in America's often good but tradition-enamored schools in a time of economic and social change deserve better treatment than that publication gave them. They also need time and opportunity to refashion their classroom practices to fit a different world and to take advantage of newly conceived styles of teaching and learning—issues I will discuss in Chapter 8.

The almost universal misinterpretation of SAT scores and international test results is evidence that we Americans need to reconsider our definition of education. As a nation we clearly have a tendency to regard schooling and education as synonymous and test scores as a measure of both. We must come to realize not only that many test scores are unreliable measures of schooling but that education involves far more than schooling. Its motivational aspects in particular are powerfully influenced by circumstances and conditions outside the school as well as within it. The problems that these outside forces create for education cannot be solved by any formulation that purports to build human beings by raising their scores on standardized tests.

2

Families, Communities, and Children

Proposals for improving the level of learning of American students by reforming the schools leave out of consideration the undeniable fact that the schools cannot do it alone. Children are all of a piece. Thinking about them as having a school life and an out-of-school life, as if these could be considered separately and had nothing to do with each other, is ignoring reality. It is either naive or irresponsible to ignore the connection between children's performance in school and their experiences with malnutrition, homelessness, lack of medical care, inadequate housing, racial and cultural discrimination, and other burdens. And blaming the schools for the results of such burdens makes as much sense as blaming medical schools for the high mortality among black babies born in American cities.

The assumption that to raise our academic achievement we must simply change the schools is wrong for all kids, not just for those from disadvantaged families. Young people in our society generally see less of their parents and other adults today than in earlier generations. Across the board in American society, we are eroding the intergenerational exchanges on which maturity is successfully built. The schools, no matter how much we reform them, cannot make up for the support children are losing because of changes in families and communities.

Families and Learning

A brief, incisive analysis of the relationship between families and learning appears in a pamphlet entitled *America's Smallest School: The Family*, published in 1992 by the Educational Testing Service (ETS). As I noted in Chapter 1, students' social background has a powerful influence upon their performance on tests. The ETS analysis gives specificity to that generalization by exploring the elements within homes that detract from school learning (such as TV watching, poverty, and absence of a parent) and the elements that have a positive influence on school success (such as home libraries, reading at home, parental involvement in schools, and adequate family resources). It also recognizes the significance of "the love and attention children receive, the security they feel, the encouragement they get to learn, and the attention given to their health."[1]

It is not possible to make a definitive statement in mathematical terms about the extent to which family circumstances dictate success or failure in school. The relationship of school to family is complex, and outcomes for individual students cannot be predicted. There is a substantial chance that a child from a poverty-stricken, single-parent, minority family will not be successful in school. The fact is, however, that some such children do succeed. Also, some schools have better records than others in helping children from disadvantaged backgrounds defy the odds.

How should educators and policymakers respond to this situation? Should they take the position that because some schools are successful with some children who carry the burdens of a negative prognosis, the basic problem is with the schools, and that therefore we should fix the schools? Or should they argue that we should directly attack the conditions of poverty and family disruption so that children will have the home support they need to be successful in school? The only possible response to these questions is that both strategies must be followed at the same time. Unless we recognize and pursue both, we will fail the coming generations of children and youth.

The school reform movement has had a strong tendency to choose the first of the above options, a choice that amounts to focusing on cure and ignoring prevention. We need to work toward preventing difficulties in the lives of children and their parents rather than putting all our energy into devising expensive ways to counteract the effects of those difficulties after the damage is done. The contrast between prevention and cure has been well expressed by Emory Bundy:

> There was an ancient Cornish custom used to test whether a person was insane. The individual was confronted with three elements: a spigot, a bucket, and a ladle. As water flowed from the spigot into the bucket, he was instructed

to keep the water from overflowing. No matter how tenaciously and effectively he ladled water from the bucket—keeping it from overflowing—he was judged insane if he failed to turn off the spigot!

By that ancient standard we behave in a crazy way, picking up the pieces of damaged children—at a greater and greater cost to society, with more and more dire consequences—rather than curb the supply. What is it in our character—in the way we organize and represent interests in this democratic society—that causes us to treat the consequences of damage far more vigorously than undertakings to prevent it?[2]

A commitment to tackle all the social problems that keep many youngsters from learning would be a daunting challenge. Its costs and its difficulty should not be underestimated. Certainly it sounds simpler to focus narrowly on fixing the schools so the schools can fix the children. But no amount of school reform will turn children into enthusiastic and successful young scholars if they come to school already badly damaged by family circumstances. There will always be a few who shine in spite of the odds against them, but a few is not enough. In the long run, ignoring the need to improve conditions for families will be more costly to our society than taking steps to improve those conditions.

The families concerned are not just those found near the bottom of the social pyramid. Middle-class families, too, have to some degree suffered from the many changes in family organization and routine in recent years, and their children, too, are finding learning more difficult. There is no question, however, about what our priorities must be in the challenging task of providing improved education through both families and schools. We must focus first on those who find themselves left out of the American dream. Otherwise we will face dire consequences from an increasingly alienated and discouraged segment of society that can disrupt civility for everyone. When persisting economic tragedy and social segregation create a core of people without hope, the American dream can seem so unattainable that it awakens little aspiration and an overdose of rage.

The well-known sociologist James Coleman has given us a useful term for the mixture of human relationships and opportunities on which children and youth depend for successful growth to maturity. He labels them "social capital" and argues that the steady decline of this resource in American families and communities is a major factor in the failure of some of our young people to become responsible adults:

> What I mean by social capital in the raising of children is the norms, the social networks, and the relationship between adults and children that are of value for the child's growing up. . . .
> Altogether, the social capital in family and neighborhood available for raising children has declined precipitously. The cost will, of course be borne by the next generation, and borne disproportionately by the disadvantaged of the next generation.[3]

The loss of social capital has come about for many reasons as our society has changed. The growing numbers of mothers who work outside the home, the climbing divorce rate, the increase in the number of single-parent families, and even the expanding amount of time family members spend watching TV instead of talking with one another—these and other trends have meant that adults have less time to spend with children and youth and that the time they do have together is often less rewarding for both parties. Coleman suggests that we invent new institutions to compensate for the shortcomings of families, institutions to provide qualities and experiences now in short supply for many children: "attention, personal interest and intensity of involvement, some persistence and continuity over time, and a certain degree of intimacy."

Fragmented Services

The call to improve schools, on the one hand, and to foster healthier families and communities, on the other, is largely a call for activity on the part of government—federal, state, and local. Unfortunately, government attention to these issues is fragmented among many different agencies; there is no single central source of funds and planning. Federal agencies that administer programs to sustain families' health, income, nutrition, work opportunities, and housing are separated both from one another and from the programs at all three levels of government that affect schooling. These agencies often deal with the same families, but they do so through different funding streams and separate offices. In general their staffs don't know about one another's activities and see the other agencies as rivals for money provided by Congress or the state. The organization of the Congress itself perpetuates this separation of services as chairs of separate committees and subcommittees focus on their narrowly defined responsibilities. A Select Committee on Children, Youth and Families in the House of Representatives, which was chaired in 1992 by Representative Patricia Schroeder of Colorado, offers a ray of hope for comprehensive thinking, but it has no role in either the framing of new laws or the appropriations process and must work through other committees to carry out its recommendations. The House Committee on Education and Labor has not shown much interest in consulting with Representative Schroeder or her equally able predecessor, George Miller of California, on new legislation.

Within states a similar situation exists. In state legislatures and in their administrative departments it is assumed that families and children can be divided into functional segments of schooling, job preparation, housing, health services, income maintenance, and the like. In the provision of social services for mental health, for youngsters in trouble with the law, for family problems like child abuse and battering, and for students rejected by schools there are frequently separate specialized activities without coordination and often without knowledge of one another—even though particular families may be afflicted by several of these problems.

With the main funding for social services provided by states and the federal government, it is not surprising that the local delivery of services to families should be segmented to fit its fiscal origins rather than family needs. This system leaves the schools, which on average draw about 94 percent of their funding from state and local sources and only 6 percent from Washington, very much on

a track of their own. Schools tend to be relatively uncon-
nected in their policies, planning, and daily routines to initiatives that might help families to become effective
educational agents in the lives of their children.

These observations on the lack of connection and coordination among the many agencies that serve families and
children are hoary, boring, and correct. They have been
around for years, and most people with serious interest in
improving the fortunes of families in need are tired of hearing them. Efforts have been made at both the federal and
state levels of government to do something about them,
often without positive results. But there is a recent and
refreshingly vigorous effort to take on these issues at the
local and, sometimes, state levels. Political rigidities are
less likely to get in the way locally, and easy local access
across agency boundaries creates opportunities for action.
As a result, recent years have seen numerous experiments
in improved cooperation among both public and private
agencies serving families, children, and youth.

The San Diego public schools are well known for a major
effort in this realm; I will have more to say about it later in
this chapter. Numerous school systems are seeking ways to
get health services into schools so that children and parents
can have easy access to them. There are some experiments
with bringing multiple services into the schools. While efforts
of this kind are generally thought to be most needed in poor
neighborhoods, there is reason to believe that they should be
considered in all schools. For example, in a recent survey in
St. Louis, one in five teenagers from the upper income group
cited unmet needs for help with problems in their lives.[4]

The idea of better-coordinated public services for families

FAMILIES, COMMUNITIES, AND CHILDREN

and children is a concept whose time has come. It has growing support at the state and local levels, and some national
programs are beginning to make their regulations more flexible, so that their support at the local level can be more useful
to enhancing the educational potential of families.

Some of the state-initiated efforts are particularly interesting. Table 1 gives the basic elements of such programs in

Table 1
Two state programs to enhance the educational potential
of families.

Minnesota:

1974—State legislation authorized six Early Childhood Family
Education sites under the State Department of Education.

Purpose—To enhance the competence of parents to provide the best
possible environment for the healthy growth of children from birth
to kindergarten enrollment.

Eligibility—Voluntary program open to expectant parents, grandpar-
ents, foster parents, and others with responsibility for children
under five years of age.

Funding—Initially from the state. Changed to combined state and
local school district in 1986, when 70 school districts participated. By
1989–90, 340 districts had the program and total expenditures were
over $23 million.

Staff—Must be licensed as "parent educators" or early childhood
teachers.

Services—Weekly classes for parents and children (separate); home
visits; special events; access to toys and books; newsletter; social services for immigrants, single parents, and teen parents.

Participation—Average participation is 35 percent of all those eligible in a school district. Some districts reach 90 percent.

Evaluation— Under way. Legislature has granted funds to extend the programs of parent education to K-3 in ten demonstration sites. State is exploring parent education for K-12.

Missouri:

1981—Started its Parents as Teachers experiment in four school districts.

Purpose—To provide parents with information and guidance to assist child's physical, social, and intellectual development; to reduce stresses and enhance pleasures of parenthood; to minimize the need for expensive remediation and special education services.

Funding—Initially local and federal money. Some private funding. State funding added in 1985–86 to join with local funds; $13 million from state in 1990–91.

Participation—All school districts in the state are required to offer the program; parents attend voluntarily. Special efforts are made to enlist at-risk families.

Staff—Parent educators must complete a required program of pre-service and in-service training.

Services—Home visits; group sessions; screening for children to determine physical, cognitive, and language development through age four; "drop-in-and-play" times; toy and book lending libraries; newsletters; referrals for special problems.

Evaluation—Evaluations have shown gains for both children and parents and some evidence of improved test scores in grade one. More comprehensive evaluations are under way.

Source: Harvard Family Research Project, *Pioneering States: Innovative Family Support and Education Programs*, 2nd ed. (Cambridge, Mass.: Harvard Graduate School of Education, 1992), pp. 16–26.

Minnesota and Missouri. A number of other states have reviewed these programs and developed their own versions for helping families to function as educators. For me, these initiatives hold great promise. No doubt course corrections will be needed as their strengths and weaknesses are explored in an orderly fashion. But they are encouraging steps toward a prevention-oriented approach to the problems that plague our families and therefore our schools.

Poverty

More and more children in the United States are living in poverty. Many of the circumstances that affect children's readiness to learn are profoundly shaped by poverty. I quote from *America's Smallest School*: "American families differ widely in their incomes and therefore in the resources that they have to support the development of children. To the extent that resources in the home account substantially for children's success in school, the unequal funding of the family school is a source of inequity in student achievement."[5] The phrase "family school" refers not to the school attended by the children in a family but rather to the educational institution that the family itself is and must be. In Chapters 4 and 5 I will discuss the unequal funding of public schools for students from poor families as compared to those for the well-to-do. Here I am concerned with the family as an educational entity.

The ebb and flow of the annual income of families with children in the United States is, to some degree, an indicator of the capacity of those families to support their children in a manner that builds success in learning. And the record shows that between 1973 and 1990 the median real income of families headed by a parent under age thirty fell by 32 percent. The poverty rate among these same families over the same period grew from 20 percent to 40 percent; for single-parent families, it grew to 50 percent. Among older families with children, the median income declined by only 6 percent, while families without children gained 11 percent. Hidden in these numbers are much higher poverty rates for young black and Latino families.[6]

Why is it that low-income families tend to have children who get low scores on tests, whose achievement as measured by teachers is lower than that of wealthier children, and who are much more likely to drop out of school before high school graduation? This question is much debated among social scientists. Studies of "family processes" have shown that factors like the style of parenting (authoritarian versus joint decisionmaking), the openness of communication between children and parents, parents' expectations of their children, and the amount of encouragement children get from parents have significant effects in all families, regardless of socioeconomic status. One interesting finding is that both "positive extrinsic reinforcement (rewards for school improvement) and negative extrinsic reinforcement (penalties for unsatisfactory schoolwork) are correlated with lower grades," while only encouragement appears to be associated with higher grades.[7]

Such research, as it becomes more certain of its conclusions, may well arm educators with findings that can be used in schools as well as in programs like the Minnesota and Missouri examples described in Table 1. But it seems to me that there are many ways in which poverty must influence children's performance in school regardless of family processes.

Consider these facts about families in poverty: Poor children tend to get inadequate medical care. Many often go hungry, and some are undernourished. Many do not have adequate shelter that allows reasonable privacy, and many live in neighborhoods that do not offer opportunities for healthy and stimulating recreation. The schools available to them are often badly underfunded compared with those available to middle-class families. Many poor families lack adequate day care, and children are sometimes left on their own in potentially damaging circumstances. A high percentage of minority people are in poverty (although more whites are on welfare than any other group); families that are both poor and minority face a dual burden of inadequate living conditions and discrimination.

Given all these disadvantages, the opportunities of parents in poor families to nurture their children and show them affection can be hampered by the demands of keeping the family afloat economically. Even when health care and other services are available, the fragmentation of services means that parents often must deal with many different bureaucracies to claim the services for their families, with all the waiting in line and other frustrations that dealing with bureaucracies entails. Because of the pressures under which they live, poor parents may falter in important parental roles more often than parents in easier economic circumstances. It should be obvious that the combination of all these factors must have a detrimental effect on families' ability to support their children's learning.

There are no complete solutions to poverty in a society, but there are ways to live with it much more constructively than we now do, to alleviate its effects, and to move more of the poor to economic self-reliance. Most of the countries that we see as troublesome competition in the international marketplace have more humane and more effective safety nets for their poor citizens than we do. Consequently their poverty rates are lower. For example, in 1988 about 17 percent of U.S. children were living in poverty, as compared with about 10 percent in West Germany and 5 percent in Sweden.[8] Could it be that their social insurance programs, which include health care, day care, and income guarantees, help to make their workers more effective parents than ours, as well as more efficient workers?

The Family Support Act of 1988 is coming into operation as I write this book. It is a potentially valuable piece of legislation that offers the unemployed training for work, day care during training, and Medicaid coverage throughout training and beyond. It holds the promise of improving the lives of many of America's poor, but the fulfillment of that promise depends upon the states and federal government acting together to finance it. The tragedy is that we haven't the political will to provide the funds that would bring the new legislation into action in a major way. A by-product of doing so would be the development in many families of a growing capacity to help their children succeed in school.

In connection with the implementation of the Family Support Act, each state has to develop its own plans within the broad parameters of the legislation. Research supported by the Rockefeller Foundation in the 1980s uncovered some priorities that have been tested in four experimental programs to help low-income, minority, single mothers prepare for and get jobs. With this kind of guidance to states, there is at least a good chance that the state-developed programs will have more success than have earlier efforts to move single parents to being self-supporting.[9]

A particularly appealing and relatively new strategy for dealing with some aspects of poverty is illuminated by a small-scale project in Massachusetts called The Right Question Project, Inc.[10] Its purpose is to increase the capacity of low-income parents to organize and take action for the needs of their children. It offers carefully prepared programs to help poor people to be politically effective in dealing with the agencies that are supposed to serve them. It is concerned with voter registration, with effective lobbying, and with learning who makes decisions that affect children, gaining access to those people, and asking them "the right questions." Essentially it is an empowering exercise that believes in making democracy work at the grassroots level. Health services, schools and school departments, and other agencies have heard from it. No doubt there are many similar community-based efforts around the country.

We have a number of very effective child advocacy groups in the United States that are mainly focused on poor children. Their role is an important one. What these people do is to harass school superintendents, political leaders, and service providers about fairness to children. The best-known such enterprise, the Children's Defense Fund headed by Marian Wright Edelman, refuses to accept public money for fear of reducing its ability to bug the bureaucrats. In the 1970s the child advocacy groups across the country formed a coalition for joint action known as the

National Coalition of Advocates for Students. With support from major foundations, this Boston-based outfit has become a vigorous voice for the special needs of poor children and their families.

A simple generalization about the healthy and successful development of children in poverty can be distilled from all the research done on their needs and problems: *The earlier and the more comprehensive the interventions made on their behalf, the more likely their success.* We know that adequate prenatal care makes a major difference; we know that balanced nutrition for mothers and young children does the same; we know that early attention to health problems can often lead to their solution; we know that orderly and well-planned experiences in peer groups can lead to socialization that undergirds school success later on.

We also know two important and disheartening facts about child poverty in the United States: that since 1980 the proportion of children living in poverty has grown from about one child in six to one child in five; and that the single largest source of this increase has been the decline in effectiveness and funding of government-supported programs in pulling families out of poverty.[11]

What happened to American children in the Reagan and Bush years in terms of federal programs for child and family health, family income, special services to children like Head Start, and other sources of support is that they were ignored. As a result the haphazard programs that served their needs declined. In 1989 the governors and the President awakened to this fact, and they put as first among their national goals for education the pious statement "By the year 2000 all children in America will start school ready to learn." As of 1992 an oversupply of rhetoric and a considerable amount of analysis of the problem had accumulated, but nothing much had been accomplished. The National Task Force on School Readiness sponsored by the National Association of State Boards of Education issued in December 1991 a publication entitled *Caring Communities: Supporting Young Children and Families.* Bill Clinton, then governor of Arkansas, chaired the task force, and both its rhetoric and its recommendations are sensible, even compelling. It recommends, in orderly fashion, attention to all the needs of children and families mentioned or implied in this chapter. What is more, it assigns specific agenda items to parents, local communities, voluntary agencies, and local, state, and national government. Nowhere have I seen a better organized document. Both Bill Clinton and Hillary Rodham Clinton are steeped in the best thinking about this topic. With Bill Clinton as President, I can't help speculating (and hoping) that their new leverage on the political processes of our country may get us moving from rhetoric to action. After all, we Americans don't deny children health care and other necessities out of any dislike for the young. We do it because our thinking about kids is muddled. Leadership committed to giving kids a better chance in life may be able to straighten out our thinking.

Communities

The family and the community are interdependent. Families can be helped to overcome their problems and to provide stronger supports for their children by a community that encourages all kinds of institutions to serve both parents and children. When social scientists attempt to analyze the strengths of a community for supporting kids and families, they include the combined roles of churches, schools, social service agencies, job placement services for teenagers, playgrounds, libraries, day care services, minority-run organizations of all kinds, health services, organizations like the Girl Scouts, boys' clubs, and the YWCA, resources for juvenile offenders, adult education opportunities, and organizations of people who live in public housing to maintain and protect their surroundings. Every place with the right to use the word "community" to describe itself needs a rich mix of these elements for its families and children. In addition, as I have said, these organizations, whether they are maintained by public or private funding or both, will meet their goals more effectively if they know about one another, exchange information about clients they serve in common, and have some capacity to jointly assess unmet needs in the community.

The Twentieth Century Fund recently recommended that all towns and cities create local boards to oversee the relationships among the many services to children and youth in each community. The new boards would identify gaps in services, promote coordination, and discourage costly duplication.[12] There are numerous examples around the United States of community-wide efforts of this kind. Some focus on all children and youth. Others concentrate on the early years of childhood. Seattle has brought youth into both the planning and the operation of new projects to serve their needs. Pinellas County in Florida has a low-level property tax to provide resources for youth services there.

FAMILIES, COMMUNITIES, AND CHILDREN

New Beginnings in San Diego is a collaborative project of the public schools, the city and county, and the San Diego Community College District.

Before New Beginnings started its activities, it took a careful look at one elementary school area that was densely populated by people from several ethnic backgrounds. It found that many families are unaware of services and their eligibility for them, that families need help in order to get help, that families often need help from several agencies, and that social workers can get discouraged by the heavy demands made on them. Faced with these findings, New Beginnings staff first analyzed the spending of each agency on services to families in the area. They call this approach "the gut level of restructuring and reallocating public funds to one interagency system."[13]

In writing about these programs through which communities can pick themselves up by their bootstraps and help families and their children to better lives, I do not mean to imply that the new systems are easy to start or are a solution to all the problems of young people. Neither is true. Much voluntary time and effort on the part of busy people are needed. Results are a long time coming and often less dramatic than hoped. Getting any value from such endeavors takes years, not months, of constant course corrections. The leadership task of maintaining optimism while the daily routine is filled with frustration, and even failure, is daunting. Sometimes the public relations announcements designed to get local support for such programs can become an embarrassment because results don't match promises. But in spite of all these qualifications, determined civic leaders are beginning to see signs of progress.

Needed: A Moral Crusade

Our government's tendency to define education narrowly and to ignore the need to improve social and economic conditions for millions of children shows up starkly in a comparison of two pamphlets about children in the United States. The first is an issue of the *ERIC Review*,[14] published by the U.S. Department of Education's Office of Educational Research and Improvement in 1992. It is about the readiness of young children for schools and how it can be achieved. The other is *Child Poverty in America*, published by the Children's Defense Fund in 1991.

Reading these two documents one after another is confusing because they appear to be about different countries. Although it concerns children's readiness for school, the *ERIC Review* never mentions the word "poverty," let alone examines the ways poverty reduces the educational effectiveness of families. Nor does it mention race and the differing circumstances of black and Hispanic families as compared to whites. Commenting on "readiness," it says, "The main issue debated is the extent to which development and learning are determined by biological and maturation processes versus experience." For me, this observation comes dangerously close to raising the nature/nurture issue and suggesting that those who aren't ready for school may be inherently without that capacity. ERIC gives us a polite, wordy, school-based document with sentences like this one: "Interactionists take the position that inherent maturational processes and experience interact to contribute to children's learning and that virtually all human beings are born with a powerful built-in disposition to learn."

Child Poverty in America, in contrast, tells in detail the story of growing poverty in the 1980s among children and young families. It connects that story to the future prospects of children. A sad but true quote from that account carries the essential message: "*The New York Times* reported on July 6, 1990 that the White House (Domestic Policy Council) acknowledged that a major new 'investment in children' would have a big payoff for Americans in the long run, but it shelved the idea after concluding that it was not likely to show an immediate reward."[15]

The people who work in the Department of Education's Office of Educational Research and Improvement are not stupid. They know that a major obstacle to readiness for school is growing poverty among children and their families; they also know that a high proportion of children in poverty are black and Hispanic, Asian and Native American. Isn't ignoring race as a significant factor in the lives of poor children an omission that borders on racism? And isn't ignoring the devastating impact of poverty on the level of learning in our country a self-defeating national policy? This pamphlet from ERIC is another in the long series of examples of how those who are supposedly our nation's educational leaders choose to focus narrowly on schools and avoid even mentioning the broader aspects of children's lives that have at least as much impact on what children accomplish in school.

Why is it that we Americans allow our leaders to ignore conditions under which more and more of our children live? Why don't those conditions spark widespread outrage that would lead to social change? For significant social action, two elements are needed: a rational understanding of the problem and a moral viewpoint to encourage change in the direction in which rationality points. In spite of the labors of those few, like Marian Wright Edelman, who combine the moral and rational approaches to the issues, we do not have a dominant moral crusade for poor children. But we do certainly have sufficient social science analysis to justify such a crusade.

Sometimes I wish that our able social scientists would learn to preach as well as to analyze. One of their great predecessors, Gunnar Myrdal, to some degree developed that dual role in his massive work published in 1944, *An American Dilemma*. Here is a paragraph from Myrdal that is worthy of our attention:

> Though our study includes economic, social, and political race relations, at bottom our problem is the moral dilemma of the American—the conflict between his moral valuations on various levels of consciousness and generality. The "American Dilemma" referred to in the title of this book is the ever-raging conflict between, on the one hand, the valuations preserved on the general plane which we shall call the "American Creed," where the American thinks, talks, and acts under the influences of high national and Christian principles, and, on the other hand, the valuations on specific planes of individual and group living where personal interests; economic, social and sexual jealousies; considerations of community prestige and conformity; group prejudice against particular persons or types of people; and all sorts of miscellaneous wants, impulses, and habits dominate his outlook.[16]

Myrdal's two-volume work was subtitled *The Negro Problem and Modern Democracy*; this quotation referred to white Americans' internal conflict over how to treat black

Americans. The dilemma Myrdal defined is still with us, as he predicted it would be, and the moral conflicts he described apply not only to relations between races but also to the way well-off Americans think about poor Americans. I believe our failure, as a nation, to recognize, become outraged over, and act to change the appalling conditions under which so many of our children are forced to live still has much to do with racism, as well as with a general tendency to let what Myrdal called "personal interests" and "economic jealousies" win out over our "high national principles."

A word of warning about the nature of change in schools, communities, and families. Even when enough moral conviction can be summoned to press for well-thought-out change, these institutions always find change difficult and accept it slowly. In a factory, a new technological development can bring sudden and useful change. Not so with the institutions that influence human beings. Attempts to change institutions that in turn must change the behavior or attitudes of human beings run into traditions, emotions, and loyalties that are very powerful in preserving the status quo. It's like changing churches—a slow game!

This is one reason educational reformers must be wary of quick fixes like school choice. But the need for wariness doesn't justify ignoring the possibility of successful change. Social change requires careful thinking about what to do and long-term commitment to doing it. Frequently there is a long period after a change is launched before the evidence is in about whether it is successful. And success is likely to require numerous adjustments in what was originally planned.

The Head Start program illustrates these points. Most of the evaluations of Head Start in the late 1960s and early 1970s showed no significant positive results for children as they moved from preschool through the elementary grades. In the early 1980s, however, longitudinal studies began to find gains in learning and school adjustment for students who had participated in the program. By the late 1980s the evidence was even stronger. Some seventeen years of follow-up of Head Start students began to show them as more successful in school, more likely to go to college, and less likely to drop out of school than students who had not been in the program.

These days, enthusiasm for Head Start is so high that it illustrates another characteristic of social change, the tendency to see anything that works as a cure-all. The fact is, of course, that many youngsters who participate in Head Start end up in jail, drop out of school, and fall for drugs or irresponsible sexual relationships or both. Head Start does not overcome all the accumulated effects of poverty and racial discrimination. Indeed, there is growing evidence that some Head Start programs just don't work because of problems such as weaknesses in leadership and poor staff performance; like any other organization, Head Start works well only when it is run well. The best we can say is that Head Start programs hold the potential to give children a better chance in life. As Marian Wright Edelman has pointed out on many occasions, the evidence we have suggests that when used effectively every dollar spent on Head Start will save more than three dollars of public expenditures on social problems in the future—not a bad investment.

Political and business leaders who see Head Start as a

cure-all fail to recognize that the same kind of support it can provide to preschool youngsters and their parents is really needed throughout the years of schooling, not just for kindergarten readiness. The governors and the President who made the first of the six National Education Goals "All children in America will start school ready to learn" said nothing about maintaining that readiness in ensuing years. They did make their sixth goal "Every school in America will be free of drugs and violence and will offer a disciplined environment conducive to learning." I very much doubt, however, that the interpretation of this goal will lead to family and community changes that could really bring it about. We are still wedded to the concept of dealing with problems of drugs, delinquency, and dropouts much too late. Effective *preventive* programs for such social ills involve a coming together of schools, families, and communities that remains rare today.

Head Start is just one example of a great variety of interventions now attempting to build into children a combination of physical and mental health, constructive attitudes and behaviors, and personal skills ranging from strong performance in school to responsible dealings with peers and adults outside it. Many of these well-intentioned endeavors have only limited leverage on the prospects of disadvantaged children because the intensity of their impact and the length of time devoted to them are inadequate to overcome the pernicious effects of disadvantages that start with prenatal development and are reinforced throughout childhood and youth.

Recent thinking about this discouraging state of affairs suggests that a much more comprehensive approach to positive interventions is needed, an approach that pays attention to the total environment of the child in preschool years and beyond, in the family, in the community, and in the school.[17] When the agencies that serve children begin to work together in a manner that makes the total effect greater than the sum of its parts, we will be likely to succeed with many more of our children than we do now. This is the challenge that faces us as we move to the next century. It is a much greater challenge than simply improving the schools.

3

Race, Culture, and Education

The narrowness of America's definition of education is starkly apparent in the national educational goals agreed upon by the governors of the fifty states and announced with considerable fanfare by President Bush in 1989. Those goals, in abbreviated form, are as follows:

By the year 2000

1. All children in America will start school ready to learn.

2. The high school graduation rate will increase to at least ninety percent.

3. American students will leave grades four, eight, and twelve with competency in English, math, science, history, and geography, able to use their minds well, and ready for responsible citizenship, further learning, and productive employment.

4. U.S. students will be first in the world in science and mathematics.

5. Every adult American will be literate enough to compete in a global economy and to exercise the rights and responsibilities of citizenship.

6. Every school in America will be free of drugs and violence and will offer an environment conducive to learning.

Although these are worthy goals (except for number four, which is unrealistic for reasons I explained in Chapter 1), all but the first ignore the part of children's lives—and their education—that takes place outside of school. What is more, they omit from the concern of schools the most pervasive social issue our country confronts: the increasing diversity of our population. Their lack of attention to this important matter reminds me of the mountaineer who arrived at the base of Mt. Everest but had forgotten his climbing boots.

As a nation of immigrants, the United States has always been a somewhat diverse society, and in recent years it has become much more so. Traditionally, the image we used to portray the blending into one nation of people of many different national backgrounds was the melting pot. We saw our newly arriving immigrants as people with the potential to become Americans by learning English, adopting our customs, abandoning their native traditions, and learning the rules of baseball. We believed that with hard work and dedication they could accomplish these tasks in a generation or two and become real Americans, indistinguishable from the rest of us.

The requirement to become indistinguishable from other Americans was a fatal flaw in the concept of the melting pot: it left out blacks, Native Americans, and a considerable portion of Hispanics. To put it bluntly, we were willing to melt culture but not race. Today, because of the progress made by the civil rights movement and because of the vast wave of immigration in the second half of the twentieth century, there has been a significant shift in our country's perception of itself. We have started to move away from the myth of the melting pot and toward a new perception of pluralism that honors our differences rather than seeking to erase them. This new concept will be a far better way to think about our differences as we become even more diverse in the decades ahead.

This increasing diversity and our attitudes toward it have immediate and powerful effects on the schools. Our educational system, whether prepared for it or not, faces and will continue to face a knotty set of problems that are becoming knottier every day because a growing proportion of our citizens, our work force, and our students in schools have racial and cultural origins that are not white and European. The avoidance of the issue of diversity by the framers of the national educational goals makes it clear that although our national self-concept is changing it still has quite a distance to go.

As the backgrounds and outside-of-school experiences of schoolchildren become more and more varied, schools must come to understand and work with the differences along with emphasizing the commonalities. Perhaps even more important, schools must become places where children from widely different backgrounds learn to respect one another and to work together. Unless the educational institutions of this country can devise both curricula and direct experiences to help young Americans to understand those who are unlike themselves—and to understand also that human beings from different backgrounds have much in common—those institutions will fail to produce the mature citizens we need. Indeed, this goal of social maturity as a challenge to our schools and colleges seems to me just as important as the goal of higher levels of learning to improve economic competitiveness—maybe more so. A crucial part of social maturity is the ability to get along with the other members of society. Unless we can maintain a sense of mutual respect and a tone of civility in our dealings with one another, successful economic competition abroad will be worth little as we attempt to maintain social peace by putting one another in jail—a remedy to which we have increasingly turned.

Racism, Discrimination, and Change in the Schools

So far our efforts to turn our schools into places where young people learn about and begin to understand one another have been only partly successful. Up until 1954 it was illegal in our southern states to have blacks and whites attend school together. In that year the *Brown* decision of the Supreme Court wiped out such legally required segregation, but the removal of the requirement didn't change the practice of the schools. Black students continued to attend black schools even though the laws creating those schools had been disallowed. In addition, many northern cities maintained "de facto" segregation—separation of the races without overt public action but with the support of well-hidden initiatives from both public and private sources.

I found myself engaged in the 1960s as U.S. Commissioner of Education with responsibility for giving federal money to public school systems under the Elementary and Secondary Education Act of 1965. To qualify for the money, school systems in both North and South had to show they were desegregated. Title VI of the Civil Rights Act of 1964 said no federal funds could go to agencies practicing discrimination, and the Supreme Court had ruled in 1954 that segregation constituted discrimination. So I had to determine when to withhold funds that school districts very much wanted. My enforcing of the requirements of Title VI led to a wave of animosity directed against me personally but based upon the feeling aroused by what some called "racial mixing," namely sending blacks and whites to school together. Attitudes that today are likely to be expressed only under the table were right out in the open back then, as a few quotes from remarks made about me on the floor of the House and Senate will show:[1]

> Howe is a misfit, a foul blot on the escutcheon of decency. This man talks like a Communist. That is why those of us who know him call him the Commissar of Education.— South Carolina congressman
>
> Harold Howe has pressed down upon the brow of the South a crown of thorns as cruel and as torturous as that pressed upon the head of the Prince of Peace when they crucified Him on the Cross.—Alabama congressman
>
> He has set out on a course of imperial threatening in the name of the Federal Government and the lash he is laying

THINKING ABOUT OUR KIDS

on the backs of the school authorities is backed by $2 billion a year of the people's own money.—Louisiana congressman

The Commissioner of Education is so ignorant he should incorporate. No one should own so much of one commodity.—South Carolina congressman

Not every voice in Congress was raised against me; just for the sake of balance, let me quote one favorable comment:

He has brought intellectual honesty, deep respect for our local traditions and enormous energy to bear on the great opportunity of our generation.—Pennsylvania senator

The threatening voices in Congress were augmented by constant harassment from the southern press. Jesse Helms, then a news broadcaster in Raleigh, North Carolina, worked me over on a regular basis. Of course I got considerable support from the northern press. But my most effective protection came from Notre Dame University. In the midst of this travail, its president, Father Theodore Hesburgh, arranged an honorary degree for me. Everyone knew that Notre Dame wouldn't give a degree to a communist. And the aura created by a connection with the nation's greatest football power provided real protective coloration. I'll always be grateful to Father Ted for identifying me with two entities Americans worship with equal vigor, God and football.

Much has changed since the 1960s. Undeniably, there have been major positive changes in the rights and the status of racial and cultural groups long denied fair treatment in America. The combined action of the federal courts and the Congress, undergirded by a vigorous mid-century civil rights movement, has reshaped the social, economic, and political roles of blacks, Hispanics, and others whose second-class citizenship had been maintained by law or overt discrimination or both. These useful changes, however, have spawned a false optimism about our success in providing equal opportunity. Today, in spite of the progress brought about by the civil rights movement, black and Hispanic communities in our cities face a crisis of staggering proportions. Racial and cultural discrimination are alive and well in the United States, although they now exist more under the table than on top of it.

A by-product of this false optimism has been the demise of the civil rights movement because the gains that have been made are falsely interpreted to mean it is no longer needed. Nothing could be further from the truth. Andrew Hacker conveys the reality of the situation as succinctly as anyone I know. He refers to blacks, but in some measure the moral issue he raises can be applied to other minority groups as well.

> A century and a quarter after slavery, white America continues to ask of its black citizens an extra patience and perseverance that whites have never required of themselves. So the question for white Americans is essentially moral: is it right to impose on members of an entire race a lesser start in life, and then to expect from them a degree of resolution that has never been demanded from your own race?[2]

Arthur Schlesinger, too, points out eloquently that our country has not overcome its history of racial prejudice: "The curse of racism was the great failure of the American Experiment, the glaring contradiction of American ideals and the still crippling disease of American life."[3] I believe that this lingering racism, though our senators and representatives no longer proclaim it aloud in the Congress, is an important factor in America's reluctance to take dramatic steps to combat poverty or to grant our inner-city (and mostly minority) schools funding more nearly equal to that of schools in wealthy (and mostly white) suburbs.

A major trend of the twentieth century in our country has been the building of suburbia outside the city. In very large part this has been a move of whites away from blacks and Hispanics, as well as a move of more fortunate people, both white and black, away from the poor people in the city. This vigorous separation of the races is seldom seen in that light. Instead it is interpreted as evidence of our growing prosperity and the success of our economic system. The people who benefited from economic prosperity demonstrated their gratitude, as well as their belief in segregation, by building public housing in the cities, not in the suburbs. They also used their political leverage to make sure that convenient roadways were paid for with public funds to carry suburbanites to work and play in the cities and home again at night.

In the mid-1970s, largely thanks to pressure from the courts, substantial numbers of black and white children were going to school together. In large cities, however, there were growing, racially isolated areas that desegregation orders from the courts could not reach. In the meantime new movements of people were changing the scene, and a large migration of minorities to the suburbs was increasingly apparent. During the 1980s, as the Justice

Department showed little interest in enforcing the law and even supported lawsuits to reduce the power of the courts to attack racial isolation, there was considerable resegregation, particularly among Hispanics. The Council of Urban Boards of Education, in a 1992 report on the status of school desegregation, painted the following picture of what the future holds for our schools:

> School officials need to accept several very important facts as starting points in plans for the future. The schools in the cities will not go back to their old enrollment patterns . . . nor will change stop now. Second, the schools in the suburbs are going to become more and more diverse racially and economically, and they will need [desegregation] plans if they are to avoid the segregation and inequality which affects the central cities. Third, planning for the future of race relations will have to come to terms with the needs and aspirations of several minority communities, of which whites may become a minority.[4]

How are the schools to deal with these changes, which have such major implications for interracial and intercultural contact and understanding? What can we do to avoid transferring to our schools the incendiary aspects of the political exchanges about racial and cultural relationships? The answers to these questions are far from simple, but I do have some suggestions.

For starters, our schools should formulate a new commitment to *making diversity work*. I would ask all those who decide educational policy to listen closely to a statement by Henry Louis Gates, Jr., chairman of the Afro-American Studies Department at Harvard University:

Ours is a late-twentieth-century world profoundly fissured by nationality, ethnicity, race, class, and gender. And the only way to transcend those divisions—to forge, for once, a civic culture that respects both differences and commonalities—is through education that seeks to comprehend the diversity of American culture. Beyond the hype and the high-flown rhetoric is a pretty homely truth: There is no tolerance without respect—and no respect without knowledge. Any human being sufficiently curious and motivated can fully possess another culture, no matter how "alien" it may appear to be.[5]

The heart of Gates's message is simply that *we need to learn about one another.* Unless we have a process for that purpose, it just won't happen. Students and teachers in every school should formulate a statement about what their school will do to help its students understand the people in it and in their country and in the world. These days teachers, parents, students, and administrators are urged to come up with a vision for their school. This concern about other people must become part of the vision. Learning about others must not be just a matter of curriculum and courses. It must involve all aspects of the school—the extracurricular activities, the role of parents, and special programs such as visiting other schools or exchanging students with them.

Initiatives toward focusing on *making diversity work* must come from both inside and outside the schools. Inside the schools, staff development programs must help teachers learn about the cultural backgrounds of children and plan teaching strategies and classroom activities to increase cultural understanding. Outside the schools, institutions of higher education have an important role to play in educating teachers about how to make our diverse society work.

Also outside schools, both political and educational leaders must accept the responsibility of breaking down racial and cultural isolation in the school. Not only is such isolation discriminatory, it is also a firm basis for building a nation of militant self-centered minorities rather than a nation of people who value one another's differences. Governor Lowell Weicker of Connecticut made a courageous step in the right direction in early 1993 when he called for a total redrawing of boundary lines for school attendance to reflect the positive purpose of getting to know one another.

Long before the cold war began to thaw, American students were engaging in exchanges with Soviet youngsters. Even then it was easier to arrange that step toward understanding than to bring kids from Scarsdale and Harlem together. Crossing the bridge from rural isolation to the central city may be even more difficult, but it can be done. Communities like Springfield, Massachusetts, maintain K-12 programs of volunteer community service for children and youth that have a strong potential for building interracial and intercultural experiences. Some youth corps programs emphasize the bringing together of young people from differing economic and social backgrounds. The possibilities are legion. But there are many schools that have no serious agenda in this realm and no organizational structure to create one. Some educators regard such activities as a waste of time and money because they don't raise the test scores.

Although some schools are coming up with encouraging ways to help students from diverse backgrounds understand one another, the nation at large has shown a disturbing tendency to set aside any interest in school desegregation. The fact is, of course, that the unanimous *Brown* decision of 1954 still stands; many large school districts are operating under court orders because of it. More than 250 school districts enrolling more than two million students operate today under court orders resulting from lawsuits brought by the Justice Department.[6] But most studies of school reform simply do not mention desegregation as a tool for improving schools. A revival of interest in school desegregation could get some support for school improvement from the federal courts, which have now instituted a doctrine of special financial assistance for schools that suffer from racial isolation that cannot be changed by legal attendance requirements. In effect the courts are saying, if we can't break down segregation we can at least make sure that those who suffer from it will get good schools. David Tatel concludes a trenchant analysis of this situation with a statement that cries out for attention from governors, business leaders, and other self-appointed saviors of schools whose vigorous participation in school reform never touches upon racial and cultural isolation in America:

> As we move toward the twenty-first century and our nation becomes increasingly diverse, the argument for integrated schools becomes more, not less, compelling. For this reason, advocates of school desegregation and school reform must work together to demonstrate to the courts that high quality, integrated schools can be maintained without perpetual court supervision.[7]

Multicultural Education

The real battle in the schools over the topic of learning about one another focuses on the formal curriculum and the related preparation of teachers. The forces engaged in that squabble range from elementary teachers, who have found that they need to know something about the cultural traditions of Southeast Asian children in order to work effectively with them, to university professors in the liberal arts, who fear that attention to the many cultures now found in the families of American schoolchildren will dilute the mainstream of western European culture that has long dominated the curriculum in our schools and colleges.

An important third party in this contest for control over time and subject matter is made up of the cultural groups who want the schools to pay more attention to their own history, literature, and traditions. Blacks in particular have understandably pushed for more recognition of their historical origins in both the United States and Africa.

In fact they have been pushing for decades, and with good reason. I recall an incident from the 1960s that illustrates the shabby treatment blacks have received in school curricula over the years. The Reverend Adam Clayton Powell, a popular and controversial black New York City congressman, was chairman of the House Committee on Education and Labor when the Elementary and Secondary Education Act (ESEA) was passed in 1965. Because ESEA provided money for schools to buy books, he decided to hold a hearing on what American textbooks had to say about such subjects as slavery, the Ku Klux Klan, and the lynching of black Americans, as well as the economic and social status of black people in America more than ten years after the *Brown* decision. In early 1966 he summoned to Washington a number of publishers and authors for a hearing before his committee to examine the content of textbooks on American history. He had carefully underlined in their books the sections about these aspects of black life in America. The books had been written to avoid offending whites in the South, so that slavery was described, for example, as "a useful and humane way to care for the needs of simple people who would be lost on their own in the complex American scene." Similar rationalizations characterized the other topics I have mentioned.

Chairman Powell always presided from a raised dais to allow him to look down on his supplicants. At this hearing, he would read from a textbook a few vapid statements about conditions among blacks in our society, and then, fixing the publisher with a gimlet-like eye, he would say, "Mr. Publisher, do you believe what this book of yours says?" It was a most effective hearing.

Of course, this use of the Congress of the United States to clear up the dirty work of racists in the publishing business, whose love of the almighty dollar exceeded their interest in truth, was not really the best way to get more accurate texts for schools. But Powell made a powerful point about the amoral business practices of the textbook world. And by implication, he also made a point about the guardians of history in universities and colleges. Where were those defenders of academic freedom as young Americans were being bamboozled in classrooms into accepting a false interpretation of the lives of their forebears?

Today, of course, blacks are far from the only group working to have their history and culture treated more fully and more accurately in the schools. What has emerged is a major movement in schools, school districts, state departments of education, and teacher training institutions that is described by the awkward phrase *multicultural education*. As this movement has grown and prospered, curricular changes have been sought with two main purposes in mind—to help children in a given school to understand one another, and to help children in all schools to understand better the history of the country that is now theirs, including who oppressed whom and when. Multiculturalism is intended to teach children about the different experiences that lie behind America's different cultures, languages, religions, and skin colors.

Multicultural education was not launched as an effort to dislodge the western tradition from our school curriculum. It recognizes that the American definition of human rights and the traditions of our democracy have long been part of a core of benefits that people from other countries come here seeking; and it recognizes also that these precious if elusive privileges are now becoming the birthrights of those who had been denied them in this country since their ancestors were brought here as slaves or converted to second-class American citizenship by force of arms.

Some tension is probably inevitable, however, between those who support multicultural education and those who see our nation's future mainly in terms of customs, values, beliefs, and traditions that come to us by the familiar route of Greece, Rome, the Middle East, Medieval Europe, the Renaissance, and a special connection to British law and governance. This second group can easily become resentful of efforts to introduce new elements into the traditional sources of school curriculum.

Those new elements are here as the result of the

growth in our Hispanic, Asian, and black populations, and of the wave of immigration in the second half of the twentieth century. And even more significant in their impact on the school curriculum have been the liberating effects of the civil rights movement and its attendant guarantees of the rights of all categories of people regardless of race, religion, national origin, or sex. For groups that have long been treated as second-class citizens, an easy and rational transition can be made from the idea that they now have equal rights and opportunities to the idea that they also have the right to seek national recognition and respect for their culture, the right to see their traditions take a place beside the traditions of others who have come to America.

The myth of the melting pot still has militant supporters today, supporters who see the new doctrine of cultural pluralism as a threat to American society. They fear it will transform our nation into a collection of competing groups striving to get ahead of one another economically and politically and feeling no sense of responsibility for one another. They fear it will damage the central core of American beliefs and values that hold us together through our Constitution, our commitment to democracy, and the common experience of our country's growth and development over several hundred years.

Arthur Schlesinger, Jr., argues this point powerfully in *The Disuniting of America*, the same book from which I quoted admiringly earlier in this chapter. Schlesinger raises the question: "Will the center hold? or will the melting pot give way to the Tower of Babel?" The bottom line of his answer is stated in a few sentences from his final pages:

RACE, CULTURE, AND EDUCATION

It has taken time to make the values real for all our citizens
... If we now repudiate the marvelous inheritance that history bestows on us, we invite the fragmentation of the
national community into a quarrelsome spatter of enclaves,
ghettos, tribes. The bonds of cohesion in our society are
sufficiently fragile ... that it makes no sense to strain them
by encouraging and exalting cultural and linguistic
apartheid.

The American identity will never be fixed and final; it
will always be in the making. Changes in the population
always brought changes in the national ethos and will continue to do so; but not, one must hope, at the expense of
national integration. The question America confronts as a
pluralistic society is how to vindicate cherished cultures
and traditions without breaking the bonds of cohesion. . . .

Our task is to combine due appreciation of the splendid
diversity of the nation with due emphasis on the great uni-
fying Western idea of individual freedom, political democracy and human rights. . . .

"What then is this American, this new man? . . . Here
individuals of all nations are melted into a new race of
men." Still a good answer—still the best hope.[8]

Schlesinger makes it clear in the book that he believes the
disintegration of our society is well under way in our
schools and colleges. It is this belief that leads him to his
strong reassertion of the value of the melting pot myth.

I believe Schlesinger misjudges the situation. American
society can absorb the challenges he identifies without losing its essential core of values. For one thing, a very large
segment of his argument is based on the exaggerated ideas
of fringe groups of black "scholars" and black activists,
some of whom want to have black students study only black

traditions. I put the word "scholars" in quotation marks because it is abundantly clear that a few students of racial and cultural history have not arrived at their interpretations through what most academics would call scholarship. They have instead manufactured history to support their positions, and their work will not stand up against competent historical analysis. But when we make such assertions we must remember that this is exactly what white historians have long done to blacks, as Congressman Powell so powerfully demonstrated in 1966. In saying this I am not advocating that we accept questionable historical interpretations, but I am suggesting that there is room for more patience and understanding in these matters than has been demonstrated by many white scholars.

Furthermore, the recent history of racial and cultural minorities in the United States clearly shows their growing success in making use of the central values and customs of our society rather than forming themselves into separate "enclaves." The growth of minority political leadership is phenomenal at every level from the town or city to the state and on to the national government. This is not a move toward separateness; it is rather a demonstration of learning how to gain participation and power by using the governmental institutions we have inherited from European sources and adapted to our own purposes. Black and Hispanic school superintendents and school board members are an integral part of our educational leadership.

Third, any long-term assessment of the economic attainments of minority groups shows genuine progress. More and more blacks and Hispanics are working beside whites in offices, factories, and other well-paying workplaces.

These gains should not blind us to the urgent needs and economic misfortunes of minority groups, difficulties that are based in part on discrimination. But compared to the situation in our country before World War II, minorities have made a significant move into the middle class and into better-paid jobs. This kind of change suggests that our society is unlikely to suffer the kind of disintegration that Schlesinger holds out as a reason for renewing our commitment to the melting pot.

Finally, Schlesinger misinterprets the dangers of linguistic diversity. There is simply no reason to think we are about to become a "Tower of Babel" or "exalt . . . linguistic apartheid," whatever that means. There are plenty of problems we should give attention to in the realm of language, such as adult literacy, teaching kids to write, raising the literacy performance of schools, helping new immigrants to learn English. But the American version of the English language is not endangered and is very unlikely to be. English is a growth stock all over the world, even in Japan. Its acquisition is high on the priority list of all immigrants because it is a necessity for employment. We could help them to learn it more effectively than we do, but that's a matter of our political will to appropriate money and not a serious threat that some other language will be imposed.

Schlesinger's discussion of bilingual education is unfair to that complex topic. Where teachers are well trained in bilingual methods, students learn English faster and better and also retain their native language, a gain in places like Florida's Dade County and southern California, where many jobs require both Spanish and English. I have seen no evidence that multicultural education seeks to prevent the

THINKING ABOUT OUR KIDS

learning of English, but it does hold out the possibility that teachers will understand their students better and that students may learn why their fellow students demonstrate unfamiliar ideas and behaviors.

My own sense of the future of American society is that diversity that allows a common core of American values to persist is the flag we must fly. As our society becomes more and more characterized by people from differing backgrounds, it is likely that the ideas of some of its diverse groups will eventually become part of the common core, but it is also quite likely that a major element of that core will remain, as it has been, a product of western civilization. The concept that should dominate our thinking is not the melting pot, with its built-in failure for racially identifiable groups. Instead we should emphasize the idea that all of us have something to learn from one another. Just like the melting pot, this idea can be only partly achieved, but it is a *positive* idea that doesn't ask people to abandon their own concept of who they are. Instead it invites them to add to it. To today's more self-conscious minorities the message of the melting pot is that their culture is second rate and expendable, and that they must adopt ours. Multicultural education is one way to convey a new and more constructive message.

In the task of making our diversity work all the institutions in society have a role—the school, the family, the community, religious organizations, private membership groups, and the workplace. For a diverse society to function well, highly conscious and regular attention to learning about others is required. As students and teachers continue to define the meaning of multicultural education, they will

RACE, CULTURE, AND EDUCATION

be helping to hold our society together. It is only the fringes of the diverse groups that threaten anarchy, and we should not let their narrow views push us into a social emphasis that is on its way out.

In the world today overwhelming numbers of nonwhite peoples with varied cultures are pressing for economic and political changes that will bring them closer to opportunities in life that resemble the American dream. As changes in technology link all people closer together, our country has the opportunity to become a laboratory for experimenting with the challenges of making diversity a positive element in the process of living peacefully together. If the melting pot remains our defining symbol, however, many outsiders looking at the United States will continue to see a society in which people like them are undervalued and often discriminated against.

It may even be that to a certain extent the melting pot myth *causes* groups to settle in the "enclaves" Arthur Schlesinger is worried about. Blacks, Hispanics, Asians, and others huddle together in our cities. Portuguese sections of cities in Massachusetts are common. Couldn't part of the reason be that they stay close together in order to avoid being consumed in the melting pot? They want to keep their culture, and flocking together makes that easier and in their view safer. If we had a social system built on the assumption of respecting the variety of our diverse groups, wouldn't people feel more comfortable about living next door to members of other groups?

Our schools today are struggling to change to meet the needs of the twenty-first century. Our government leaders have set educational goals for that purpose without mentioning the persistent tensions that defeat progress toward social fairness. By this omission they accept a narrow definition of knowledge. In effect they say that knowledge about the cultures of people who will eventually constitute a majority in our country is not important.

Henry Louis Gates, Jr., punctures this narrow concept of what is worth knowing by citing a verse composed by students of the great Victorian classicist Benjamin Jowett. Gates says the doggerel "nicely sums up the monoculturalists' claims":

> Here I stand, my name is Jowett
> If there's knowledge, then I know it.
> I am the master of this college
> What I know not, is not knowledge.

Gates goes on to counter this narrowness of vision in a way that eloquently sums up the points I have been making in this chapter:

> Ours is a society that simply won't survive without the values of tolerance: and cultural tolerance comes to nothing without cultural understanding. In short, the challenge facing America in the next century will be the shaping, at long last, of a truly common public culture, one responsive to the long silenced cultures of color. For if we relinquish the ideal of America as a plural nation, we abandon the very experiment that America represents. And that, surely, is too great a price to pay.[9]

4

Choice: The Millennium?

The school reform movement in the United states is rife with millennial thinking. The word "millennium" has come to mean a time of great happiness, a time when human ills disappear, a time of good and successful government. An educational millennium is a period during which our highest hopes for education are realized, when children learn what they are supposed to learn and schools are clearly successful institutions. Not surprisingly, millennial thinkers are susceptible to overly rosy predictions for the future. Tending to believe a certain policy will solve all problems and issue in a utopian era, they often do not base their recommendations on any solid evidence of what works, and they fail to think through all the difficulties of the plans they propose.

These tendencies are reaching epidemic proportions in a major movement that is now being pressed at the center of the school reform agenda: the idea that all students will learn better if parents are given a *choice* on where their children will go to school. Some advocates of choice believe it should apply to public schools only. Others would extend it to private schools as well; federal legislation to achieve that purpose was introduced into the Congress when George Bush was president.

Why do I believe the advocacy of choice as the solution to our country's educational problems is a good example of millennial thinking? First of all, there is very little hard evidence about what the effects of a system of choice would be if it were universally installed in American schools. What positive evidence there is about school choice has come from much more limited programs that tell us little about how nationwide choice would work. I will have more to say about some of these smaller programs later in this chapter. There is one recent major analytical book on this subject, *Politics, Markets, and America's Schools* by John Chubb and Terry Moe,[1] but the experiments from which the authors drew their evidence were few in number, limited in scope, and tested over a relatively short period of time. Chubb and Moe recognize that choice has some inherent difficulties, but they nevertheless espouse it lock, stock, and barrel.

My second reason is that the most eager advocates of school choice have been leaders in the business community and the Reagan and Bush administrations, along with right-wing policy analysts—people who know little about schools and schooling and who propose the concept as the way into a total revolution in the organization of schools. Starting with the idea that choice of schools by parents is an expansion of freedom and therefore inherently a good thing, these enthusiasts present an argument that goes as follows:

CHOICE: THE MILLENNIUM?

The eighth wonder of the world is the capitalist system of economic organization. It has brought more good to more people than any other large-scale human social invention. Therefore its basic assumptions are to be treasured and transferred to all possible realms of human activity. Test scores show that our schools are mired in mediocrity, if not in failure; it is time to let the schools benefit from the capitalist assumption that competition produces quality. When parents can choose schools, schools will compete with one another to attract students. The better schools will succeed, and the students will emerge from them better prepared to work in the factories and offices of the capitalist system. The bad schools will lose business and wither away, as Marx argued that the evil state would wither away, and the good schools, along with those which change from bad to good in order to survive, will dominate the educational scene. The wonderful power of competition to produce quality will solve all the messy little problems like how to pay for schools, find and prepare good teachers, and motivate children to learn.

If this isn't millennial thinking, I can't imagine what is.

This position is based on some assumptions about education that I have already shown to be questionable. One is that American schools are no good because SAT scores have gone down and American students score below those of other nations on international tests. As I pointed out in Chapter 1, the main factor in the decline in SAT scores is the change in the social and economic backgrounds of those taking the tests, and international comparisons of test scores are unreliable because of differences in the groups of students tested. Also, test scores are powerfully influenced by cultural, social, and economic factors in addition to schools, particularly the increase in the number of children living in poverty. Even for the narrow goal of raising test scores, therefore, the validity of school choice as a central strategy for reform is dubious at best. If we think with realism rather than millennially, it is clear that we must tackle the dual task of working on family and community as well as schools if our efforts for children are to succeed. None of the advocates of competition has yet suggested that students should be able to choose their families to bring the benefits of competition to the home.

Another assumption of basic choice theory, one I have seldom seen questioned, is that competition always produces quality. My own observations on this issue do not stem from the study of economics. But in more than seven decades of living in the United States I have found the cherished practice of competitive business a doubtful purveyor of benefits in many situations.

I happen to subscribe to a magazine for consumers. Each month there appears a long list of unsafe cars, toys damaging to children, household machines with electrical hazards, and chemicals devised to improve life that in fact threaten it. Along with these products of competition comes another list of untrue and misleading advertisements urging people to invest their money in doubtful ventures or to acquire credit cards charging exorbitant interest rates or to buy the defective or unsafe items on the first list.

While I am quite aware of Better Business Bureaus and other efforts to put voluntary bounds on the negative aspects of competition, I doubt that human beings can ever adequately control the power of human greed, which is given free rein in a competitive system. It is universal, and it tarnishes our lives every day. A competitive educational system would require a vast new system of regulation to see that schools, in their competition for students, did not hide mediocre quality behind misleading advertising. Once schools were on a competitive basis, how would prospective parents ever get truly objective information about them?

Even a casual examination of the wonders of competition in American business in recent years raises doubts about its capacity to produce quality. The vast automobile industry spent decades producing inferior vehicles and propping them up with giddy advertising. True, Japanese competition eventually awakened the automobile companies, but can we wait that long to rescue our children?

Furthermore, the education of children is a fundamentally different enterprise from the production of cars or any other large-scale profit-making endeavor. We have already been through in this century an era of school organization for which the factory was the model. That model is responsible for the lock-step, inflexible organization of our schools as well as for the idea that children are like gadgets on an assembly line. Move them along, give every one the same treatment, and you'll produce a useful product. Not a bad idea with candy bars or washing machines, but a disaster with human beings, about whose development in their early years we now know vastly more than we did when the factory model of schooling was devised.

A major effect of competition is to make agencies that compete want to keep their secrets of success from one another. In competitive business some policies, procedures, and activities are jealously guarded to make sure competitors cannot benefit from them. This is true of football teams, electronics manufacturing, the fashion industry, and a host of others. Do we really want to encourage schools that develop successful ways of dealing with children to keep those ways a secret? How would that tendency affect the connection between schools and universities seeking research opportunities for improving schools? I believe the present emphasis on openness about what works and what doesn't is an important positive element in the nature of schools. I am not saying that competition necessarily prevents openness, but it does cast a shadow on it that is not in the spirit of the value system I see as desirable for educating children. It would be a sad day for education if schools began to patent or copyright successful teaching strategies to stave off competition. And if the high stakes of school survival and job continuity became part of the daily routine, teachers would be less enthusiastic about going to professional meetings and sharing their own experience with colleagues. They would prefer to stay home and focus on boosting their students' test scores. Whether or not the tests involved have educational value for the students, higher scores will attract parents.

A case can be made that competition brings out both the best and the worst in us. In sports, where it is usually seen as a positive element, competition produces both the desire to excel and an equal desire to break the rules in order to beat the other guy. We tend to disapprove of the pitcher who has some sandpaper in his glove to rough up the ball, but we also admire his ingenuity. The famous football player who carried a knife, deflated the ball, and ran for a touchdown with the ball flattened under his jersey is a folk hero. The Rugby School in England has a monument inscribed to honor the player who, "with a fine disregard for the rules of the game, first picked up the ball and ran with it, thus creating the great game of rugby football." Breaking the rules of sport is considered an honor; getting caught is the sin. Apparently that's the way it is, too, with banks and savings and loan companies in the United States. Do we want to run our schools that way?

As I have said, flawed assumptions underlie the push for a sweeping change to school choice. But even if those assumptions were accurate, a move to completely free choice would bring endless problems and questions. Some of these are fiscal in nature. If a student who lives in district A decides to attend a school in district B, how will the student's schooling be paid for? Should district A be required to transfer to district B an amount equal to district A's per-pupil cost? Or if the per-pupil cost of the new school is 30 percent higher, must district A come up with the full amount? Would that be fair to district A's schools and taxpayers?

State funds are distributed under formulas that provide different amounts per pupil to school districts, depending upon each district's property tax base: the richer the district, the less money it gets from the state. If a student in Chelsea, Massachusetts, which gets the highest state funding per pupil, decides to go to school in Lexington, which gets one of the lower per-pupil allocations, should the state pay wealthy Lexington the same amount it would have paid Chelsea for that student? Under a choice system, wouldn't students from poor districts with high state payments tend to move to high-cost suburbs with elegant schools and less money from the state? And wouldn't districts with vacancies recruit them to get the relatively high state payments? There is a kind of bounty-hunting element in some of these possibilities.

It also seems likely that districts with low per-pupil costs would be seriously hurt by transfers based on choice. When even a few students leave a district, say three students from each of its eight schools, the district's total costs are largely unaffected. But if the district's per-pupil cost is $6,000, it loses $144,000 if the per-pupil costs are transferred. Only if all twenty-four students were in the same grade and class could the district realize some savings to balance the loss, and even then it would lose major amounts of overhead costs, which are not affected by the change. And if the students were leaving the district to attend schools in richer districts, the transferred funds would be taken from the poor to give to the rich.

The poorer districts might lose more than just money to the wealthier districts. A *Boston Globe* editorial in 1991 pointed out another danger:

> It is widely believed that under a choice system, the flow of students would be from urban school districts to more affluent school districts.
>
> If a choice system let the receiving districts simply take the very best students from the urban districts, it would have the pernicious effect of increasing the concentration of problematic students in the urban districts, reducing the revenues available to those districts, and exacerbating the educational inequality between urban and suburban schools.[2]

Besides the financial effects on school districts, there is the question of who gets the right to choose a different school and who doesn't. The glib answer of advocates of choice is that of course every family with children in school would have the right to choose. This optimistic response overlooks some basic truths. Having a *right* to do something means that you can indeed do it if you wish. But most choice options that now exist depend upon the student's ability to get to the new school the parents have chosen. Particularly if the new school is in another district, the family must provide transportation—usually from the boundary of the original district. Changing schools within a district also often requires family-provided transport. Sometimes low-cost tickets for public transportation are made available—but they aren't much use to children in kindergarten and the early grades. In other words, if you own a car and have an available adult or teenager to provide transportation twice a day, you can exercise your right to choose a school. At a time when a high percentage of parents are working and poverty is growing, these qualifications make a mockery of freedom of choice.

Another barrier to true choice is the question of whether there are places available in the school to which parents want to send their children. School enrollment ebbs and flows with population shifts, birthrate fluctuations, and economic development. So it is difficult to predict when and where schools might have available space that would allow parents to exercise choice. An overview of school enrollment in the United States for the years immediately ahead suggests that space will be limited. According to the Census Bureau the population in the age group from birth to age seventeen was 64.4 million in 1990 and is predicted to be 64.9 million in 2010—not a huge increase, but enough to make school vacancies rather scarce. If space is available in certain areas because of economic depression in a community, or because many students have transferred out in search of better schools, the schools parents are free to choose may be those that are ill-supported and in trouble.

What kind of choice system would be fair—fair to school districts and to families? The same editorial in the *Boston Globe* that pointed out how choice might hurt poorer school districts offered some guidelines for fairness that make sense:

> However the number of places for students is determined, the receiving district must fill those slots on some random basis without regard to the educational challenge a given student presents. If such a system would require the state to give the receiving districts extra funds because a particular student's education is especially costly, so be it.
>
> An elaborate—and probably expensive—information system has to be established so that all parents in participating school districts can be made aware of the educational offerings in districts elsewhere. Absent this, only families of means with the flexibility to travel around could assess the opportunities available.
>
> The plan must include transportation, and the state will probably have to pay the tab. Again, if only those who have the ability to transport their children to other districts could participate, the plan would be fatally flawed.

Even if we were to devise and institute a choice plan that everyone agreed was fair, it might well have disadvantages for the quality of education. We know from reliable research that schools with a strong connection to parents, so that home and school become an alliance to encourage learning, have a good chance of producing academic success. Children learn well where parents become partners with teachers and students in making the school a true community, where people know one another, share planning and decisionmaking, and build an atmosphere of mutual respect. These relationships take time to build. Choice will have a negative effect on them if parents are less likely to participate in a school where they have no community connections, or in a school district where they aren't eligible to vote. It also may be more difficult for parents to get to such a school to visit classes and meet their children's teachers.

As a nation we already assign far too much importance to standardized tests as measures of school quality, and the choice movement is likely to reinforce that kind of unhealthy thinking. Under a competitive system schools will surely use test scores erroneously to describe their quality and therewith to attract parents. To judge the real quality of schools we must evaluate carefully not just academic outcomes but also those having to do with human values. We must look for schools that emphasize not only academics but also qualities like respecting others, caring for those in need, helping others learn, and working in groups rather than just for individual achievement. In all the hours of debate I have heard and all the tracts I have read supporting choice, there has been almost no mention of such matters.

To the millennial thinkers school choice has great appeal. It seems to require very little in the way of additional tax money. It promises to fix everything through the wonder of improved quality created by competition. The superficial

attraction of these seemingly simple adjustments is powerful. Political leaders and business magnates who want better schools are easily sold on the idea that this is the way to
get them. After all, for them the prescription of choice and
competition offers an ego trip: "Be like me and you will be
successful." The only business leader I know who has seriously questioned the clamor for choice is Owen B. Butler,
former chairman of Procter and Gamble, who raises some of
the issues that concern me. Here is some of what he has to
say on the subject:

> School choice is a tempting idea. As a veteran of more than
> forty years in corporate America, I strongly believe in the
> benefits of competition and free enterprise. But schools are
> not businesses and students are neither products nor con-
> sumers. Including private schools in the choice system may
> be a good idea, but it may also be a very bad idea. The prob-
> lem is we just don't know. There are a number of issues
> that need to be addressed before we leap on this band-
> wagon.[3]

How far has the choice bandwagon traveled to date?
Since the mid-1980s various aspects of choice have been
endorsed by state legislative actions. By 1991 more than
twenty states had laws allowing secondary school students
to take college courses, and a few allowed use of school
funds to do so. Such programs make great sense to me as
additions to the flexibility of schools in meeting the educational needs of some of their older students. But this kind
of choice doesn't involve a focus on competition among
schools. At least six states have approved the choice of
schools outside the students' own school districts. A few

states have launched educational clinics for dropouts or to prevent dropping out, a strategy that resembles the alternative school concept of earlier years. But in all these new initiatives there are substantial limits on choice.[4]

Some limited applications of choice have had good results. Two communities near where I live, Acton and Cambridge, Massachusetts, have allowed limited choice for a number of years and found it satisfying to students, teachers, and parents. But their use of choice has been very different from what the basic theory proposes. They have used it mainly as a device to offer variety in the routines and basic assumptions of teaching and learning, thus allowing parents a choice of educational style—traditional, progressive, and so on. The school districts have not shut down "bad" schools. There is no Darwinian assumption in the school systems involved. Also, particularly in Cambridge, where there is a substantial minority population, choices have not been allowed to create racial or cultural isolation in a school. Parents do not always get their first choice because of the importance of preserving diversity in each school. Yet parents appear to approve and value the arrangement. Teachers value it too, for the variety of teaching environments it offers. This type of choice seems to operate reasonably well. But it won't sort out the bad schools as the theory suggests, and choice is restricted to situations when there is room for it in the chosen school without creating racial imbalance. Programs in effect elsewhere also place limitations on choice—in order to maintain integrated schools, or because of transportation problems, or for fiscal reasons.

School choice, in some form, is probably here to stay. In

the coming years it will probably continue to move forward in the models that now exist and even some new ones. Before he became president, Bill Clinton supported choice, and he will probably continue to do so. But he knows enough about schooling issues to be aware that choice will not usher in the millennium. School choice will probably open up improved opportunities for a few youngsters who are lucky enough to have alert and action-oriented parents: for example, in New York City's plan to launch a number of smaller secondary schools, each with its own creative theme, enrollment will be limited by the capacity of the schools, so parents will have to act quickly to get their children into the schools they prefer. But there is little reason to expect that choice will soon or ever have revolutionary effects on the quality of schools by eliminating weak schools and bolstering others. That kind of expectation constitutes the millennial aspect of the program.

With all its problems, choice is also a vehicle for what some of its strong supporters see as a moral issue. If rich people can have a choice of schools, they maintain, that privilege should be available to all families. This is the position of Jack Coons, a law professor at the University of California at Berkeley. Coons has led campaigns for ballot proposals to bring choice to California schools, but these have been defeated partly because of organized opposition from teachers and partly because of the complexity of the proposals themselves. This complexity grows from the issues that must be faced if choice is installed, particularly its likelihood of increasing racial and cultural isolation in schools.

Unlike the many supporters of choice who naively see it

as a cure-all, Coons is a thoughtful and determined advocate under the banner of fairness. He considers choice an opportunity that all families should have, just as they should have the chance to select good medical care. He is aware of most of the difficulties I have outlined about choice and believes they can be dealt with and ultimately solved. His is a voice that those of us who are skeptical about a universal choice system need to hear.

More listening to one another by the participants in the debate about choice would be a good thing. We don't know enough about the pluses and minuses of the proposed choice programs to make firm judgments about their value. The various patterns of choice now emerging in school districts and states across the country provide the laboratory we need to learn more about it. If we can stop rushing toward some illusory millennial solution and if the ideological enthusiasts can quiet down so that a really searching conversation can take place, we will be far more likely to end up with a program or programs that are good for the students in whose interests we are supposedly having this debate.

5

Does Money Make a Difference?

Questions of how much money is needed to give children a good education and where the money should come from are never long absent from political debate. In recent years a new slant on the argument has appeared: the contention that money is not the answer at all, that appropriating more funds for education would be a useless exercise in "throwing money at the situation." This idea is handy for those more interested in cutting spending than in aiding children.

The recognition that education is not just a matter of schooling makes the question of how much money is needed to support it discouragingly complex. Children's success in school is tied to their opportunities in families and communities and to their health, nutrition, housing, recreation, and chances to associate with adults in constructive relationships. How can we ever put a reasonable price tag on all these factors that undergird a child's education?

The answer is that we can't. What we can do, however, is to divide the question into more manageable segments by listing some major aspects of children's lives that need attention from local, state, and national sources of public funds. Obviously, children and families in poverty have many such needs, as I have already discussed in Chapter 2. But the need for more outside-of-school funding to help children succeed in school does not suddenly stop as we cross the poverty line. Instead, it tapers off gradually as we move upward in the socioeconomic pyramid of American society. A recent study by the William T. Grant Foundation Commission on Work, Family, and Citizenship found that there is a strong case to be made for the idea that America harbors a "forgotten half."[1] These are people who do not expect to go to college, whose opportunities for decent jobs are eroding, who may not be in poverty but certainly experience insecurity, and in whose educational future much less is invested from public resources than is true of the college bound.

Within the forgotten half, of course, are the truly poor. I have already called attention to the inadequacy of the publicly supported safety net that our nation maintains for its poor. The major feature of that safety net, Aid to Families with Dependent Children (AFDC), has steadily declined in purchasing power over the past decade. Also, the amount poor families receive from the program varies from state to state, depending not just on differences in cost of living but also on the political will of the state to match federal contributions. AFDC is in the process of being replaced by the Family Support Act of 1988. That legislation offers high hopes but limited delivery, also because of limited funding. It depends on money from each state to match federal funds. Substantial federal funds are available, but the states can't match them, because most of the states are broke, a condition that has been created by two developments: a widespread tax revolt at the state and local levels of government, and a massive dumping of federal obligations on the states during the Reagan and Bush presidencies.

What the United States clearly needs is a system of child allowances that would form the nucleus of family policy, as it does in many European countries. But such a venture is not on the agenda of either political party. Rather than building a real safety net that would guarantee decent living standards to the poor, we stumble along patching up the old one. Even considering schooling alone, we pay for this neglect many times over through children's unreadiness for school, failure in school, unreadiness for jobs, and self-destructive behavior involving truancy and dropping out, drugs, delinquency, and irresponsible sex. The real social costs of dealing with those behaviors are much higher than an investment in an effective safety net would be. Among these costs is the increase in our prison population from 240,000 in 1975 to 604,000 in 1989—a period when violent crime did not increase. We prefer to solve our social problems by putting people in jail, even though our "prison binge" costs us about $25,000 a year for each prisoner.[2]

In addition to rethinking our safety net for school readiness, we need to make better use of the incomplete collection of separate programs that now serve us for that purpose. Back in the 1970s, when I worked in the Ford

Foundation, a colleague of mine, Terry Saario, thought that Ford should invest some of its funds in understanding the problems of youth and developing information about their needs that would assist both state and national governments to design better policies to serve the young. To get started, she brought together at a series of regional conferences a cross-section of people from agencies serving children and youth. One thing we learned from the conferences was that a good many of the people working on behalf of the young in a given state had never met and were glad to have the opportunity at the Ford Foundation's expense.

In at least one of these meetings, an effort was made to discuss the total annual budget for all of the activities for early adolescents in a particular state. As this information was laboriously assembled, the men and women present became more and more surprised by the vast amounts that were indeed available annually. The question was asked, "Suppose that instead of having each item on this list a totally separate endeavor, we were able to do more comprehensive planning to meet priorities of need: would the funds be spent as they now are?" The response was a resounding negative. There followed a long discussion of the political difficulties and the turf battles among agencies that would result from any such effort to coordinate funding for youth so that high-priority needs might get the attention they deserved.

This anecdote raises the same issues mentioned in Chapter 2 about the need for more coherent planning and operation of services for all young people. This topic must stand at the top of our agenda for thinking about public funds for education broadly conceived. Unless we bring an end to the long-standing fragmentation of programs and funding, there is a good chance that the limited funds we have will be used for low-priority purposes.

In July 1992 I testified at a hearing of the Senate Committee on Labor and Human Resources, chaired by Senator Edward M. Kennedy, concerning a bill that had been introduced into the Senate with the following purpose: "To amend the Public Health Service Act to establish a program to provide grants to improve the quantity and availability of comprehensive education, health and social services for at-risk youth and their families." My testimony touched on many of the themes I have already discussed in this book. Although this legislation did not pass in 1992, it was still alive and well in the new Congress in 1993 and Senator Kennedy expected it to move forward during the year.

Funding the Schools

School funding is the largest or nearly the largest item in the budgets of all towns and cities and all but one state, New Hampshire. That cranky, independent-minded jurisdiction remains in the nineteenth century in both its financing of schools and its tax system. The broad picture of school funding by states varies widely, with New Hampshire at one extreme providing about 10 percent of school costs and Hawaii at the other with 100 percent state funding. In 1989 an average of all the states showed about 48 percent of total school support coming from state taxes, about 46 percent from local property taxes, and about 6 percent from the federal government. These proportions have probably shifted today to about 50 percent state and 44 percent local.

Whatever the source of the money, states vary widely in the amount of school funding per pupil. Setting aside Alaska, where all costs are some 30 percent higher, New Jersey and New York spent over $8,000 per pupil in 1990-91, while Utah scraped along on $3,115 per pupil, Idaho on $3,118, and Mississippi on $3,128. The average of all states was $5,342 in 1990-91; today it is just over $6,000 in unequalized dollars.[3] Hidden within these numbers are substantial differences in amounts spent on schools in urban, suburban, and rural areas; within a state, some districts are likely to be funded well below the state average. With an average annual expenditure of just above $3,000 per pupil, the states at the bottom of the list have many schools trying to serve children on $2,500 per pupil or less. It can't be done. At that level, children have to be short-changed.

From time to time in the past, this inequality of expenditure has been the subject of both national debates and major proposals for change in order to provide fairness to children. In the 1950s, for example, Senator Robert Taft of Ohio, a conservative Republican, twice proposed legislation to bring federal money to public schools. He argued that they were too important to be left to the fiscal whims of states and localities. He was defeated in both efforts by two powerful forces—private, religious schools (mostly Roman Catholic) which wanted federal money too if the public schools got it, and southern political leaders, who saw federal money for schools, quite rightly, as a foot in the door for abolishing racially segregated schools.

DOES MONEY MAKE A DIFFERENCE?

Taft was followed twenty years later by the National Education Association's proposal for school funding: one-third local, one-third state, and one-third federal. This quite rational approach never got the backing of any political leader with the leverage to get it seriously considered. And, as far as I know, there is no one today either in politics or in educational policy analysis who is interested in exploring such a possibility. With the current bind in the federal budget, that is not surprising.

Considering that some states are poorer than others and therefore are less able to fund schools adequately, a reasonable argument can be made for a federal contribution to each state based on its fiscal capacity. In 1990 average per capita personal income was about $25,000 in New York and about $22,000 in New Jersey. Utah and Mississippi had $14,000 and $13,000. If the amount of money spent per pupil has any relationship to the quality of education received (a question I will discuss shortly), then children in Mississippi and Utah are being shortchanged, and those states have limited fiscal capacities to correct that situation.

Inequities in per-pupil expenditures between rich and poor school districts within states are often as marked as those between rich states and poor states. One of the main sources of funding for schools is local property taxes. If a school district has a substantial amount of taxable property behind each child enrolled, it can support adequate schools without having to tax property at a high rate. But in a school district that has only half as much property behind each child as its more fortunate neighbor, the tax rate will have to be twice as high if expenditures per pupil are to be the same.

In most states this variation in the capacity to pay for

decent schools is reduced by substantial funds paid to school districts by the state. In theory, the state's contribution should be set at a level that would raise the total funding of property-poor districts enough to provide children with effective schools. In fact, however, political demands from several sources bend the distribution of state funds to please pressure groups rather than to promote equity.

For example, schools in wealthy suburbs like Scarsdale, Wellesley, or Winnetka often manage to capture more state funds than equity considerations would justify. They have a generous amount of property evaluation behind each child, perhaps even enough to forgo any state funding and still have good schools and reasonable property tax rates. But that is not the way taxpayers in these communities see it. Their sense of fairness starts with what they see as their heavy payment of income and other taxes into both the state and the city or town. These communities have more leverage on political decisions about state money than their voting numbers would suggest because they harbor more than their share of influential people. Over the years the annual gravy from the state has been institutionalized into the very high per-pupil expenditures in which their school districts luxuriate. Therefore, they interpret the potential reallocation of state funds to needier districts as an infringement of their rights and a threat to the quality of their children's schooling.

The result is a distribution of funds for supporting schools in the United States that is to a large degree upside down. The families with the greatest capacity to enrich all the aspects of their children's education that take place outside of school also benefit from the unfair distribution of public funds for schools, so that the school districts with the least need for state funds get more than they should.

In the school districts with much lower property valuations behind each child, the situation is reversed. Their property taxes do not yield enough funding to pay for good schools. At the same time, their families and communities are likely to be poorer and less able to provide strong outside-of-school supports for education. Although state payments for education are often larger on a per-pupil basis in such districts than in property-rich districts, they frequently are not large enough to bring high-quality schools to their children and youth.

Since the 1960s this irrational distribution of public funds to support schools has been the target of reformers. Their strategies have been mainly of two kinds: political action to add new funds to those available for the education of children who are denied adequate schooling, and legal action in the state courts to order a more equitable distribution of state funds to school districts.

School Funding in the Courts

Over the years, in accordance with the second of these strategies, a number of lawsuits have been mounted in various states to bring about more equity in funding among school districts. The results have been mixed. I served as an expert witness in a certain Texas case, which the plaintiffs won; in a case in Ohio which won in the trial court but was turned down in the superior court; and in a case in New Hampshire that was dropped because the court required the plaintiffs to reorganize their evidence in a manner that they couldn't afford (there is some reason to believe that New Hampshire's Supreme Court knew they could not afford it and used the tactic to get the suit dropped).

The Texas case has had an interesting history since the state court ruled in 1987 that the maldistribution of funds in local school districts was unconstitutional. I recall that the plaintiffs asserted that the hundred school districts with the lowest per-pupil costs spent an average of just under $2,000 per student per year, while the highest hundred districts averaged over $5,000 per student. They argued that these disparities were unfair, particularly because the student populations in the high-spending hundred districts were more than 80 percent white while those in the low-spending hundred were about 80 percent or more minority. The State of Texas argued that such differences in support of schools made no real difference in educational opportunity—the "money doesn't matter" viewpoint. Although the court ruled for the plaintiffs and ordered the state to create a totally new system for supporting schools, that order had not been carried out by mid-1993, six years later. Texas governors and legislatures just diddled around, from time to time offering inadequate additional money. The political atmosphere of Texas is such that new taxes for schools don't have a chance, even though adequate support for schools could be easily arranged without jarring Texas out of its proud position as a low-tax state. Many of its citizens are still dreaming of the halcyon days when oil wealth undergirded the cost of government. Basically, Texas wants to be a no-tax state. In my opinion, the judge should hold the legislators and the governor in contempt and stick them in jail for a while if they had no solution by the court's deadline of June 1, 1993. A more realistic alternative would be for the court to take over and run the schools, as courts have done in the past to enforce school desegregation orders.

Success in the state courts or even in federal courts, however, can result in surprises. Back in 1971, in another Texas case known as the *Rodriguez* case (named for the plaintiffs in San Antonio), a three-judge federal court supported the claim for additional state funding for poor school districts. But the defendants appealed to the U.S. Supreme Court. The plaintiffs were not seeking to promote equity in school funding for Texas as compared to other states; they were seeking to establish the right for children in different Texas school districts to have equitably financed schooling under the Fourteenth Amendment to the U.S. Constitution.

The Fourteenth Amendment, among other provisions, forbids a state to "deny to any person within its jurisdiction the equal protection of the laws." A normal person might think that states that were providing poor, black, and Hispanic youngsters with low-cost and ineffective schooling and middle-class white kids with high-cost, good-quality schooling were somehow denying the former "the equal protection of the laws." But lawyers and judges are not normal people, and they have managed to define certain categories of activities that do not qualify for full protection under the Fourteenth Amendment. Among these categories is education. The U.S. Supreme Court, by a vote of 5–4, denied the petitions of the *Rodriguez* plaintiffs and told them that Texas was treating them fairly as far as the

Constitution was concerned. The dissent on the case, written by Justice Thurgood Marshall, is worth quoting:

> The Court today decides, in effect, that a State may constitutionally vary the quality of education which it offers its children in accordance with the amount of taxable wealth located in the school districts within which they reside. The majority's decision represents an abrupt departure from the mainstream of recent state and federal court decisions concerning the unconstitutionality of state educational financing schemes dependent upon taxable local wealth. More unfortunately, though, the majority's holding can only be seen as a retreat from our historic commitment to equality of educational opportunity and as unsupportable acquiescence in a system which deprives children in their earliest years of the chance to reach their full potential as citizens. The Court does this despite the absence of any substantial justification for a scheme which arbitrarily channels educational resources in accordance with the fortuity of the amount of taxable wealth within each district.[4]

With this decision, the hope of enlisting the federal courts in fair school financing for students went down the drain by one vote. Today's court would probably defeat a similar case by 7–2, a signal of recent social progress in legal rights for disadvantaged Americans.

In the *Rodriguez* case the plaintiffs based their argument on an amendment to the U.S. Constitution. The ruling created a presumption that the Fourteenth Amendment cannot be used to bring equity to school financing. In suits before state courts, however, the basis for decisions has to be the phrasing of the state constitution. State constitutions differ widely in what they say. California, for example, has a clause on the "equal protection of the laws" like that in the Fourteenth Amendment, and the clause has been the basis for several successful suits for low-cost districts there. New Jersey's constitution requires a "thorough and efficient" education system—whatever that means. The courts have interpreted it, too, to carry a message supporting more equal treatment of students in different school districts with widely varying expenditures per pupil.

The Special Case of Special Education

Controversies over the equity of funding for schooling do not arise only at the federal and state levels. Within school districts, too, there are many issues about the fair distribution of funds, issues with no simple answers. Prominent among them is the situation created by the major national commitment to special education. The Education of All Handicapped Children Act of 1975 gave mentally and physically handicapped youngsters a right to education designed to meet their particular needs, regardless of the cost of the additional services required.

This humane and much needed legislation was not accompanied by enough federal funds to meet its costs, which on the average are nearly twice the costs of regular classes. As a result, school districts struggle to meet the imperatives of the law, which are enforced by courts when necessary. This legal leverage has forced districts, when they have been unable to get additional tax money from state or local sources, to fund special education by taking resources away from regular schooling activities. In poorer districts, this transfer of funds to special education further reduces the funding available for many students who are already being shortchanged.

An added complication—and an added cost—emerges from the tendency to assign children to special education classes just because they are not doing well in regular classes. Although they may not have identifiable handicaps of a kind intended under the law for special treatment, school authorities often feel they will be better served by the individual attention available in special education classes. Sometimes parents seek such assignments for their children.

Immense amounts of money are involved in special education, and the complexity of the situation is far greater than this brief description suggests. In cities where there are high concentrations of poor families with all the difficulties poverty creates in the lives of the young, it is extremely difficult to draw rational lines between disadvantaged children with eligibility for Chapter I funds and other children with conditions that truly warrant the much larger expenditure involved in special education. As a result, some cities have a much higher proportion of special education assignments than is warranted and carry per-pupil costs that are excessive while simultaneously denying regular classes the support required for a strong program. National experts estimate that about 10 percent or slightly less of all children should be in special education categories. This percentage is enhanced by state legislation in Massachusetts, and about 15 to 16 percent of its children qualify. In the city of Boston, however, the percentage of such children is climbing each year and reached 24 to 25 percent in 1992.

Millions of dollars are going into a form of education of

children that is both expensive and not necessarily designed to meet their educational needs. Resolving this complex dilemma will require a combination of fiscal and educational changes that will not come about easily. While there are changes that can be made in schools in the training of principals and teachers and in the way children are assigned to special education, a considerable segment of the long-term solution will lie in adequate public provision for the aspects of children's lives that take place outside of school in family and community.

Does Money Matter?

All the attempts to equalize funding for schools are based on the assumption that getting more money to ill-supported schools will help them to be more successful with their students. As I said at the beginning of this chapter, however, the simple idea that money makes a difference in the capacity of schools to serve the young is far from universally supported in spite of its rather commonsense nature. Opponents argue that there is already enough money in the schools and all we need to do is to make better use of it. The person who dreamed up the assertion "throwing money at the problem won't solve it" provided a catchphrase that has had considerable influence on reducing support for needy children, not only in schools but also in other important realms such as family support, health, and day care. This catchphrase found powerful supporters in the Bush administration, including the President himself; his Secretary of Education, Lamar Alexander; and his Assistant Secretary of Education, Chester Finn.

In general the viewpoint that more money would make

no difference is a convenient way of hiding from responsibility while superficially proclaiming sympathy, which doesn't cost anything. In many cases, I regret to say, it is also a cover for racism, since many of the young people whose schools are ill-supported are not white. Another source of this view is the belief that government action can't help with social problems, a conviction pursued aggressively only for poor children and ignored when it comes to providing student aid to middle-class college students or Social Security for well-off older people.

In spite of the widely expressed belief that money isn't needed and won't help, particularly if it comes from Washington, the largest federally supported program for education is based on the assumption that it will. Originally labeled Title I of the Elementary Secondary Education Act of 1965 and funded at about a billion dollars a year, it is now called Chapter I and provides more than five billion dollars a year to schools with a high proportion of disadvantaged children.

This add-on funding from Uncle Sam to give special help to children from poor families has now been with us for just over twenty-five years. It was made possible by a masterly political compromise that allowed the Roman Catholic Church to support it by extending its services to *all children in poverty* wherever they went to school. Funds were to move directly into public schools in amounts proportional to the number of children eligible for AFDC. Funds were also awarded for services to private school children, but they had to be delivered outside the schools, a cumbersome but politically necessary arrangement to get around the constitutional barriers of separation of church and state.

DOES MONEY MAKE A DIFFERENCE?

This major application of federal funds to help with school success for the poor should have settled the ideological argument about whether money makes a difference. The evidence from the National Assessment of Educational Progress shows that minority-group children have improved their learning levels slowly but regularly over the years since Title I was enacted. Particularly when another program for school readiness, Head Start, is added to the picture, there is little doubt that additional funds for schooling, when used well, do help.

An immense amount of social science analysis has accompanied the money controversy, some of it proving that money makes a difference and some proving the opposite. Some of the best evidence available is found in the work of Ron Ferguson of the Kennedy School of Government at Harvard. His in-depth examination of achievement test data from about nine hundred school districts in Texas clearly shows a strong relationship between dollars spent on schooling and improved achievement in reading and mathematics. David C. Berliner of Arizona State University has commented on these findings as follows:

> It is important to ask, when someone says money does not make a difference, whether the money we are talking about is for instructional purposes, such as teachers' salaries, class size, professional growth, and so forth, or whether it is for other purposes. The per-pupil expenditures for busing in rural areas, for building new facilities, for athletic programs and for other non-instructional costs, should not be expected to have direct effects on student achievement. But the money school districts spend on instructional variables, including the teachers' salaries, matters a great deal.

THINKING ABOUT OUR KIDS

Whoever says money does not make a difference has simply
not disaggregated the data.[5]

An argument can be made that American public schools
fall into two categories: (1) regular public schools that are
diminished in their capacity to promote learning by a combination of low funding and lack of initiatives to bring
about improved learning; and (2) suburban schools and a
few city schools that have enough money to do a good job
and have used that money wisely to build strong schools.
This second group of schools, at least in its suburban mani-
festation, is really a group of semiprivate schools set up and
maintained by parents who are willing to pay well for their
children's education. Instead of sending their youngsters to
expensive, truly private schools, these parents support high
local property taxes and pay their teachers well. By using
federal tax deductibility for their mortgage costs, these parents get Uncle Sam to join them in paying for schooling,
and they also get some help from the state tax system as
the state chips in for public schools and they deduct their
state and local taxes on their federal tax returns. Viewed in
this light, the school finance arrangements we have in this
country are a system for promoting better schools for the
children of the well-to-do.

The overall picture of school financing in the United
States today creates a temptation to seek some millennial
solution, perhaps going back to the suggestion of having
federal, state, and local government each pay one-third. We
might come to something like that if the American attitude
toward taxes were less negative than it now is. While there
is some hope in the state-level lawsuits that force states to

DOES MONEY MAKE A DIFFERENCE?

raise more money for schools and distribute it more fairly among local districts, there are also hard lessons about the ultimate effects of such suits. California, for example, won the struggle for fiscal equity of school districts in the courts. But then the anti-tax enthusiasts took control by passing tax-capping resolutions that limited local taxes in a manner that has seriously damaged the state's public schools. No doubt some taxpayers—but surely few parents of public school children—are happy as California has sunk to the position of about forty-seventh among the states in terms of expenditures per pupil as a percentage of average personal income. New Hampshire, of course, proudly occupies the fiftieth rung of that ladder. California's teacher/student ratios have worsened drastically as more equitable funding has been sold down the river by tax capping.

Our system for supporting the education of young Americans comes close to modeling the attributes of our economic system. It gives the best schooling to the children who already have the advantage of parents who had such schooling and the worst schooling to children whose parents are poor and ill-schooled. In effect, it is a system for throwing money at the rich to make their kids richer. And these characteristics are undergirded by the high percentage of its support from state and local taxes, which are much more regressive than federal taxes, so that the costs of schools fall more heavily on the lower income groups in America, even as their children are less well served than those in wealthier districts. In this we are consistent: we provide the least fortunate among us with second-rate police protection and limited health services in addition to

THINKING ABOUT OUR KIDS

inadequate schools, and we do the opposite for the fortunate. It is difficult to understand why the rich are so
opposed to throwing money at the poor when they throw so
much of it at themselves.

This reluctance of middle- and upper-class Americans to
pay taxes—particularly taxes to benefit the poor—is a
major reason that a real safety net for the poor on the
European model is not on the agenda of our political parties. Americans always seem to be convinced that their
taxes are already too high. It is instructive to compare the
tax burdens of the United States with those of some other
countries. The percentage of Gross Domestic Product rep-
resented by annual tax receipts offers a rough index of a
country's overall effort to deal with social and economic
issues that affect the lives of all citizens (see Table 2).
What the numbers in the table say to me is that American

Table 2
Total tax receipts in 1989 as a percentage of Gross Domestic Product (includes all state, local, and national
taxes).

Sweden	56.1
Netherlands	46.0
France	43.8
Germany	38.1
U.K.	36.5
Canada	35.3
U.S.A.	30.1

Source: OECD Statistics on the Member Countries, 1992 (Paris: Organisation for
Economic Co-operation and Development).

complaints about heavy taxation are unwarranted and that there is plenty of room in our tax system to make more of an effort for any cause we can muster the political will to address. As I noted earlier, New Hampshire is by far the least responsible state in the country in terms of providing adequate tax funds for schools and other services. These numbers show that the United States is the New Hampshire of the developed world.

As we dither along trying to boost need-based programs marginally, we continue to support efforts that don't work, partly because they are inadequately funded. After a major effort to expand Head Start, we have raised it to the level of serving about 35 percent of eligible children (President Clinton has promised to do better than that); our new Family Support Act isn't working for lack of money in the states; we have 37 million people without health coverage, a high proportion of them children; the Job Training Partnership Act serves less than 10 percent of eligible youth and young adults; Chapter I of the Elementary and Secondary Education Act does not add sufficient funds per child to bring city youngsters educational services anywhere near those typical of well-to-do suburbs. The list could go on and on.

Isn't it time for Americans to look one another in the eye and admit that the politics of getting adequate funds to help the needy aren't working? It may be that the only way to get this country to support services for children and families is to offer the services to *all* families, regardless of need. This is what we do for senior citizens with Social Security, which has become a cherished program dear to the hearts of Americans at all income levels. We are already launched on doing this in the health field. Why not day care, child support, and other significant necessities? I will return to this possible strategy in the Conclusion.

A prescient column by Fred Branfman catches the true implications of our arrangements for funding education for children and youth in both modes—inside and outside the schools:

> America needs to transfer at least one trillion dollars annually from consumption into investment in industry, the environment, schools, cities, and infrastructure to restore the promise of America for ourselves and for our children . . . We cannot increase investment without being prepared to make the kind of sacrifice for our children that our parents made for us. This requires above all a new *spiritual ethic* of concern for the generations to come.[6]

Ultimately, our choices about what we do with money come down to moral issues just as do our choices about the way we conduct our diverse society. There has been much talk recently about what we can do through education to promote the values that can preserve our basic beliefs as a nation and simultaneously address the compelling choices of a changing world. As we think about values and about funding our schools we might consider the major expenditures our country has made to equip itself with a versatile and up-to-date system for military defense. We now face a situation in regard to the future of our children that threatens us as much as the Soviet Union ever did.

6

Students Are People!

That students are people may not seem to be a great educational discovery. But it is astonishing how many school reformers ignore that simple fact. The school reform movement in the United States is heavily loaded with proposals for specifying what should be studied, for extending the time spent in school, for increasing rigor and requirements, for testing students and revealing their shortcomings, and for otherwise doing what some critic of American children and youth has described as "making the little bastards shape up." This agenda gives little consideration to reforms that would make schools more humane institutions, places as interested in helping students *grow* up as in making them shape up.

Factory Schools

Much of American education (and much of the school reform movement), particularly in secondary schools, is still influenced by the idea that schools should operate like factories, moving students along an assembly line, adding knowledge along the way, until they have a finished product and can award a diploma. Most of the organizational and educational aspects of our schools still reflect this factory model, which has characterized American schools for most of this century. The pervasiveness of this model makes it easy to forget, when we think about educational policy, that every student is different from every other, and that some students need more time or different learning strategies if they are to succeed.

When students don't succeed, our policy is to take them off the assembly line, attempt to repair their faults, and then put them back on the line until they graduate. When we find that some students can't be repaired, we do the same thing factories do. We sell them as "seconds"—damaged goods that may have some value but are not worthy of being labeled with our brand name, the diploma.

When falling test scores, rising dropout rates, and other evidence prompted many critics to proclaim that our schools had gone downhill, we wondered why our factory schools were turning out less uniform products than in the good old days. We ignored the obvious fact that the young human beings we were attempting to mold and mass-produce were themselves far less uniform than before. Much larger proportions of our children and youth were going to school, and the growing diversity of our population meant that schools served ever more varied groups of students. Our ignoring of these changes in our student population is clear from the fact that most schools have not changed much over the years. Even many of those who call for reforming the schools do not consider fundamental, institutional change. Instead they think of more ways to tamper with the components of the existing system—curriculum, testing, promotion requirements, and the like—to make the assembly line function better.

The manifesto of the first wave of school reform, *A Nation at Risk*, exemplified this tendency to impose stricter production standards instead of treating students as people. Largely in response to that document, millions of meaningless new tests consumed the time of students and teachers to little or no advantage. Those youngsters who did badly on these tests and who, along with their teachers, already knew they were doing badly, received a new and destructive infusion of discouragement in the form of low test scores followed by mindless tracking. In the name of "standards" they were taken off the assembly line and put on lower tracks for repairs—a strategy that most often failed to restore either their learning or their motivation to learn. Some cities boasted about the large proportion of students they held back in the interest of maintaining standards, even while new research was underlining the detrimental aspects of grade retention. Teachers found themselves forced to drill youngsters on exercises invented to simulate test questions instead of offering interesting and motivating experiences in the classroom. And all of this organized effort to revitalize the old model of schooling through an emphasis on "rigor" was most damaging to the children and youth with the greatest needs for recognition as people, those whose lives had been dominated by poverty and racial or cultural discrimination. We must recognize that the students in our schools are not raw material to be shaped into uniform products but rather are human beings with hopes, feelings, and ideas about themselves formed by experiences both within and outside the school. When we do recognize that students are people, we will abandon the factory system as a model for schools.

The Competitive Ethic

Another way in which our educational system is less humane than it should be, it seems to me, is in inculcating a competitive ethic that emphasizes individual achievement over cooperation and that divides students into winners and losers. Both the school choice movement, which believes competing for students will save our schools, and those who call for additional testing to compare students and schools with one another would like us to give even more emphasis to individual performance in academic tasks as the be-all and end-all of improved schooling. The more this individualistic approach to learning dominates our schools, the more some very important learning practices—and many students—will lose out.

Some dissenting voices do speak out against this focus on competitiveness. The cooperative education movement promotes the idea of learning together in groups in place of the highly individualistic competition that so often dominates a school's climate. Among other strategies, it emphasizes enlisting students to promote one another's learning and making teachers partners with students in learning rather than adversaries whose main purpose is judging students' work. Both students and teachers respond to such changes with enthusiasm, and learning is enhanced. This view of how to promote learning received some support from a recent study at Harvard University, led by Professor Richard Light, in which undergraduates testified that some of their most valuable learning experiences came from working in small groups with other students. As they saw it, the process of helping one another to understand complex issues or relationships boosted their learning.[1]

This kind of learning process is more often found in the early years of schooling than in secondary schools. It is also common in graduate schools of law, education, and business. This small-study-group approach seems to have a triple whammy. By turning students into teachers it powerfully advances their basic understanding of subject matter. By making fellow students a source of learning it builds human relationships that can both motivate learning and help students to untangle difficult concepts. Most important, cooperative learning models in the school the way people behave in the world outside the school. Teams of people working together on projects bring different talents that merge to produce a new formulation that none could achieve alone. Why do we have so little of this cooperative learning in our high schools? Could it be because each student is seen as a separate entity on the assembly line of the education factory?

Some years ago at the U.S. Military Academy at West Point, a group of cadets got together to study physics. But they were disciplined for cheating. They were supposed to do it alone, not gain from others. Then the Academy could compute a grade for each student each day and average them all up to create a pecking order that would follow the cadets throughout their military careers. What an asinine

way to promote learning, or for that matter, to build character! Students who want to help their peers should be
rewarded, not punished.

Secondary schools and colleges cannot avoid having to
some degree a sorting-out function: they must provide a
basis for identifying students with the ability and the motivation to go on to much more demanding activities that are
often selective in their admissions. But that function need
not dominate everything that happens in schools, as if
learning were like a track meet—no prizes unless you win
or place in an event. It seems to me that the academically
sacred notion of being first in the class or last in the class or
somewhere in between in the class could well be abandoned as the least useful information about students. Even
though it has some value in predicting performance in college, it tells us nothing about a student's capacity for original thinking, about his or her interpersonal skills, or about
honesty, reliability, patience, morality, or drug habits, not to
mention leadership potential. In a system of schools mod-
eled on factories, it may simply measure how well a student
manages to conform to rigid assembly-line routines.

New Directions

From time to time in the past, movements within education have come along and tried to crack the pedagogical and
organizational rigidities of factory-model schools.
Progressive education in the 1920s and 1930s tried to make
schools friendly communities for young people, particularly
those who found nothing but frustration in the lock-step
system of grades, promotions, and requirements to have

everyone learn the same things in the same length of time and in the same way. The worthy theories of progressive education, such as discovery-based learning and an emphasis on motivation, foundered partly on the rocks of ill-conceived practice and partly on the intransigent nature of the existing system. Another initiative called life adjustment education, which came along after World War II, met a similar fate. Based on the sensible theory that schooling should have relevance to the lives of learners, it lost out because of unimaginative classroom routines that sought the least common denominator of student experience.

Now here we are on the verge of the twenty-first century still dependent upon a schooling system that clearly doesn't work for a growing proportion of those we want to include in it. There is hope for the future, however, in a variety of new ventures being tried at the present time. Across the United States, educators are working on new models of schooling based on the recognition that students are people.

One of these educators is James Comer, a psychiatrist at the Yale University School of Medicine, who started to work with two elementary schools in New Haven in the 1970s. He had a simple goal: to help schools to become places where all the people involved treated one another with respect, knew one another, and felt a responsibility to make the institution they shared a friendly and stimulating place. In other words, he wanted the school to be a community in which students, parents, teachers, janitors, and the principal really felt a common bond.

This simple goal turned out to be far from easy to implement. There is nothing simple about creating a community of mutual respect out of a school where authority is frequently used arbitrarily, where students are told they are failures more often than they are praised, where parents are neither welcomed nor respected but rather regarded as intruders, and where the self-esteem of children is not considered important.

Such change is expensive, and its results are often not immediately apparent. Back in the 1970s, when I was at the Ford Foundation, I recommended tapering off support for Comer's project after several years of substantial costs. At the urging of my colleague Marjorie Martus, however, we continued support for the project, and it slowly began to show positive results in school attendance, in the feelings of adults and children about their school, and ultimately in test scores. As it did so, Comer was able to get substantial support elsewhere. In the meantime, I had received an important lesson about giving new models of education time to prove themselves. Fundamental changes in schools are very difficult to bring about. There is no quick fix.

Jim Comer made this point himself in a recent letter to me after I had sent him a draft of these pages with my confession that I had recommended cutting funding for his project in its early years:

> I . . . hope that it will help funders think about how long it takes to bring about change—particularly when we are going against the grain of traditional cultural beliefs. I shudder when I hear people talking about doing an evaluation after one year. It was seven years before the academic gains showed up in our two schools although we knew we were on the way by the third year. I hope your comments will help people begin to consider evaluation of the soundness of the theoretical construct and the quality of the implementation

as much as or more than the outcome in the early stages of interventions in complex human systems.

If schools are to fit Comer's vision of communities in which all members treat one another with respect, the adults working in them must respect the students. Young people of all ages and conditions of life respond positively to being trusted. With trust from adults they will progressively gain confidence in their ability to perform on tasks that challenge them, tasks that require growth of their abilities and their talents. When their school environment is one in which they feel genuinely respected and secure, they are more likely to be willing to take the risk of attempting learning that seems difficult.

Our large public high schools with thousands of pupils, sometimes on two sessions a day so that half the students never see the other half, are places where it is extremely difficult to build the kind of association among teachers and students that Comer's vision suggests. A teacher who has five classes of thirty to thirty-five youngsters, each meeting for forty- or fifty-minute periods, may take months just to learn all the students' names.

Some research appeared years ago on the number of pupils known by name by school principals. I do not recall the exact numbers from the study, but the findings went something like this: In a school of 300 children, a principal will know all of them by name; when the school reaches 600 children, she may know half or fewer; with an enrollment of 1,200, she may know only about 200; and the number of known students sinks further at even higher enrollments. I sometimes wonder why we have to do so much research on the subject of dropouts. Kids leave school because they don't like it, and a large part of that dislike grows from forced anonymity combined with an overdose of negative messages about themselves. There undoubtedly are some talented and dedicated school principals who stand outside the school door and welcome a thousand pupils each morning by name. But there aren't many, and there probably won't be.

When I became principal of Newton High School in Massachusetts in 1957, it had about 3,200 students in three grades. I knew very few of them. I sensed it was a school where many youngsters got little personal attention from faculty and counselors, even though it was a very well supported suburban high school with a proud record of academic success. We tried to alter this situation by starting a "house plan"—dividing the school into units of 400 to 500 students, each with its housemaster, counselors, and teachers. As much as possible we scheduled a student's classes inside his or her house. Student government and some extracurricular activities were operated on a house basis. This effort to personalize and decentralize a mass institution was partly successful, and when Newton built a new high school, it was constructed to embrace the house plan. Although the plan cost more money and created some new problems, it did result in a reduction of discipline problems, probably because the housemasters knew their students by name and because of all that such a relationship implies about lubricating the friction between the student and the school.

There is nothing novel about this strategy of restructuring organizations to create more intimacy. It was adopted by both Harvard and Yale universities in their undergraduate colleges seventy-five years ago, and it has spread to many other large institutions, both public and private. Historians of education have observed that one of the great strengths of the village school for children of all ages was the intimacy of associations within it. People gain respect for one another when they know one another well enough to break down the barriers of mutual suspicion that are created by an impersonal environment.

In the summer of 1992 the New York City public schools announced an initiative to create thirty new high schools with enrollments of 300 to 1,000 students. In 1992 New York had 124 high schools with an average enrollment of 2,500 students; some schools had as many as 5,000. The new initiative, recommended by then-Chancellor Joseph A. Fernandez and backed by the school board, is certainly a step toward changing the human environment of the schools by seeking to replace anonymity with intimacy.

Another example of efforts to create a more human environment for the learning process is found in the work of Theodore Sizer, a historian with experience in schooling and related matters. He and his colleagues have put together what they call the Coalition of Essential Schools, a nationwide network of several hundred public and private secondary schools that are attempting to make radical changes in the aspects of factory-model schooling that discourage learning. Their work is based upon an extended study of American high schools conducted from 1979 to 1984. They have no cookie-cutter recipe for bringing about change; each of their schools is approaching change in its own way. But they do offer some general principles that show their awareness that students—and teachers—are people.

One principle is that changes must be developed within each individual school by the people there, so that they achieve a sense of ownership of the change. Without this they will never become committed to the really hard work that change requires. Another is that the relationship between students and teachers must be altered: students must accept more responsibility for their own learning, and teachers must take on a role more like that of coaches in athletics. In other words, teachers must become helpers to students in finding learning, rather than its major source. In such a role, teachers learn along with their students. A third principle is that diplomas be awarded on the basis of accomplishment as demonstrated by "exhibits" of students' work, rather than on the basis of accumulated credit hours.

To make these developments possible, conditions in schools that stand in their way must be changed. Some conditions in need of revision are the student load of teachers, the system of structuring the school day into many short periods, the lack of time for teachers to plan learning activities in which students will take the lead, and classroom routines in which teachers do most of the talking. The additional costs associated with these changes will be well worth it if the schools are transmuted from places to store kids into places where exciting learning takes place.[2]

Ted Sizer's great contribution to school reform is found in his concern for what goes on in the individual classroom. He is arguing for a more motivating pedagogy than is found in many schools today, but he is doing so with the important qualification that it cannot be implanted from outside the school. Imposing "new curriculum" or new tests or additional learning time by fiat from the state or the school district won't bring the needed change; teachers have to want the change and adopt it in their classrooms. Essentially, what Sizer is saying is that both students and teachers are people, and that if we don't recognize that truth, the schools won't change very much. The struggle to implement his ideas is now under way in some three hundred schools. Their experiences over time will teach us some important lessons about American schools.

I could mention many other originators of school changes who recognize the importance of motivating children and youth. John Goodlad's book *A Place Called School*[3] provides powerful research-based support for the need to recognize that students are people. Goodlad's bottom line is that most schools are dull places for kids, partly because teachers talk most of the time while kids have to listen. He told us early on to turn that practice around, and he is attempting to do so in the two related realms of school practice and teacher preparation.

Henry Levin's formulation "Don't remediate. Accelerate" is essentially a call to capture the interest of the young by giving them challenging material to learn about rather than dull routines. He, too, presides over a growing network of schools—the Accelerated Schools Project, which expected to have three hundred participants in 1992-93. He believes that people learn best when high levels of learning are expected of them, when they see a purpose for the learning, and when what is to be learned is intrinsically intriguing. "Instead of treating students as the object of their education," he says, "Accelerated Schools should make students the subject of their own education. Schools can accomplish this by using interesting applications tied to students' cultures and their everyday experiences."[4]

Deborah Meier is probably the best-known school principal in the country for her work at Central Park East Secondary School in East Harlem in New York City. Her success in merging a deep concern for students as people with changes to make the learning process more effective is both a shining example for others and a frequently misinterpreted phenomenon. When we read about impressive successes, we are likely to underestimate how very difficult they are to achieve. Deborah Meier and the teachers who work with her have some useful ideas about how to work with young people and their families to increase school success. But what tends to go unmentioned in accounts of their work is the long hours, the frequent failures and frustrations, the battles about limitations imposed by the school district, and many other crosscurrents that typify the daily school routines. It is much easier to operate a school on the well-entrenched factory system than it is to operate one that starts from the premise that students are people.

Deborah Meier joined with Chancellor Fernandez to work on the new and smaller high schools he proposed for New York. Explaining the need for smaller schools, she has said, "Most human beings need to be known, and it is more critical when other things are also fragile . . . Kids are dying in these large schools."[5] Smaller schools do make it easier for students to be known, but it is important to keep in mind that a small school doesn't automatically produce the advantages for which it has the potential. The school principal who operates in the tradition of Genghis Khan can ruin a small school as thoroughly as a large one. And teachers in schools of all sizes need assistance with moving toward the kind of instructional practices that Ted Sizer is suggesting. The size of a school, or of a "house" or other unit within a school, can create an opportunity for more rewarding human relationships, but unless that opportunity is grasped, developed, and continually reinforced by the daily routines of the school and its classrooms, no significant gains are likely.

This short list of leading agents of change in American schools omits an army of teachers, principals, and other professional educators sprinkled around our land who are trying to make schools and classrooms friendlier and more stimulating places for students to be. It also leaves out many scholars of education who are increasingly focusing their analytical work on what happens inside schools rather than on what they can find in libraries or vast collections of computerized data. And it does not include another small army of voluntary workers in school reform who range from parents volunteering time in school classrooms to business leaders testifying in Congress about more money for Head Start.

Our school reform movement in the United States has gradually moved toward the concept of "systemic change." The term conveys a notion that everything that goes on in schools or that influences them is up for rethinking and possible change. Under its rubric the curriculum, the pedagogy, the organization, and other aspects of schools should all be considered candidates for change. So should the education of teachers, the financing of schools, and the roles of parents—to list a sample of the variables that define a school.

Even advocates of systemic change, though, often leave off of their agenda any recognition of the importance of having schools see students as people. Systemic changes such as national tests, national standards, and universal school choice for parents don't give this concept the time of day. Early in the school reform movement there was much interest in "school climate" or what was called "school ethos"—both ideas connected to motivating young people through a positive and supportive environment. But those objectives seem to have faded into the past. I have perused a number of carefully prepared outlines for systemic change in schools. Among the most comprehensive of them was one drafted by the Education Commission of the States. But none of them gave any attention to the need for human relationships in a school to be purposely considered, carefully worked upon, and continually reinforced if the school as an institution is to be successful.

If I had to pick out one set of heroes and heroines in the current school reform movement for recognition of their contribution to useful changes in the schools, I would be frustrated by having to choose between two groups: those teachers who have managed to change their classrooms into places where their students can find excitement about learning and a sense of being among friends with a common purpose; and those principals who have developed the personal skills to encourage and help teachers to reach for such classrooms amidst all the cacophony of school reform. Perhaps the basic strategy for American schools should not be the systemic changes that are so widely supported by political leaders but rather a strategy of discovering how to use the able teachers and principals we already have to help others gain mastery of their talents within the context of the individual school and classroom.

Graduate schools of education and other places where people gather to think about education are loaded with psychologists—explorers of the mind and of human behavior. Any psychologist you encounter in or near schools is very likely to be interested in something called "child development" or "adolescent development." When psychologists start to talk about development many people turn off their hearing aids or go elsewhere, but that overused word carries an important message for thinking about schools. Development usually connotes change for the better (although in universities it means raising money), and when applied to students it suggests that they are changing not only in their academic learning at school but also through the process of maturing. Youngsters change rapidly in a great many respects: in their emotional reactions and behaviors, in their social skills, in their intellectual activities and capacities, and probably in other ways that psychologists would be glad to enumerate. And, of course, the changes they go through in these realms are powerfully influenced by their experiences in homes, communities, and schools.

One good idea that psychologists have pressed upon schools is that it makes sense to have the experiences of students in school related to their developmental age—a somewhat fuzzy concept suggesting that each child grows and changes in ways that bring on readiness for increasingly complex tasks. Not all students are ready to deal with learning to read at exactly the same time or in exactly the same way, and pressures to do so can result in unnecessary failure, which in turn can be damaging. Seymour Papert, a professor at the Massachusetts Institute of Technology, has suggested that it would make sense to have kindergarten and first-grade students learn to write on a computer or even an old-fashioned typewriter and avoid the laborious formation of letters by hand, which can be learned much more easily at about age eight, when a youngster's development brings improved mind-muscle coordination for fine-tuned tasks like writing. Although this accommodation sounds sensible, my guess is that the force of tradition defeats it for most kids. So they struggle with the formation of letters and words when they could be writing stories by poking keys.

I knew a psychologist named Omar Khayyam Moore at Yale University back in the early 1960s. He had a Carnegie grant to install early-model computers in a school for the use of kindergartners and first graders. These little kids were publishing a daily newspaper for their school. He had taught them touch typing by painting their fingernails different colors and painting the keys to be touched by a given finger in the same color. I thought it was a signal of a brave new world, but apparently it hasn't caught on much.

This bow in the direction of psychologists is provided to illustrate an important general point: when schools are organized and run in ways that fit the school to both the learning needs and the developmental needs of children, both children and schools are successful; but when schools attempt to cram learning into students without regard to their developmental needs, children fail and so do schools.

This general argument is likely to be challenged under the banner of setting standards for schools. Traditionalists see standards as tasks that must be performed or skills that must be learned or knowledge that must be mastered. They would ask a youngster who could jump over a bar three feet high to try four feet and fail him if he didn't make it, when what is needed is 3'3" and some coaching.

Today's school reform movement has a habit of moving higher levels of learning downward in the frenetic race for excellence. Junior high schools and middle schools, which ought to be places for older children and younger adolescents not only to concentrate on academics but to flex their new muscles, to explore new social relationships, to find out more about the many choices their lives will bring them in the next few years, and to understand the implications of their sexual development, are pressured to ignore these developmental needs and to push students to engage in academic studies in a manner more suited to high school or even college. Kindergartens are still seen as places for social development, but even their routines are being altered by more highly structured learning.

Today some major efforts are going forward across the country to change junior high schools and middle schools to fit better with their students' developmental needs. Joan Lipsitz, whose book *Growing Up Forgotten*[6] was a seminal contribution before the present school reform movement appeared, has been a major contributor to thinking about these issues. In founding the Center for Early Adolescence in Chapel Hill, North Carolina, she created a resource for stimulating change to benefit this age group, whose schools too often are invaded by the rigidities of the high school.

In 1989 a study by the Council of Chief State School Officers "frankly acknowledged a glaring problem: most young adolescents' schools are strikingly out of phase with the developmental, social, and academic needs of these students."[7] Subsequently, twenty-seven states agreed to rethink and change their middle schools and junior highs to fit the needs of students. With help from the Carnegie Corporation, which supported the original study, these states have launched initiatives during the last three years to address the problem. They are beginning to make progress.

For too long, the schools of our country have treated students as products moving along an assembly line, or as receptacles into which teachers should pour learning and which should then be tested to see if the learning has remained or leaked out. In emphasizing that students are people I wish to encourage schools to challenge these well-entrenched patterns. If educators pay careful attention to human relationships and foster a sense of the school as a community, schools can become places where both students and teachers want to be. The promising initiatives I have described in this chapter are demonstrating not only that schools can be humane and educate well, but also that they cannot educate well unless they are humane.

7

Time: The Procrustean Bed

Theseus, a hero of Greek mythology, managed to defeat the wily Procrustes, a legendary hazard to travelers. Procrustes had an iron bed to which he lured his victims. If they were too long for the bed, he cut off their feet; if they were too short, he stretched them to fit. From this myth comes the so-called Procrustean bed—a situation that arbitrarily imposes conformity. Procrustes might have invented the factory model of schooling.

The use of time by schools in the United States is a good example of a Procrustean bed. Consider what we do to students in school even though we know they are very different from one another when they start school and will become even less alike as they pursue learning. We insist that students achieve their learning in the same amount of time, regardless of their differences. Then we tell them that those who succeed in this amount of time are worthy and those who don't are failures. This way of guaranteeing that a large proportion of students will be labeled failures is a major characteristic of factory schooling. It is seen by its supporters, however, as an element of rigor and high standards in the educational process.

Schools, Prisons, and Wine Cellars

Much of the activity of schools, and of colleges as well, is encased in time and subject-matter containers that we call courses. First-year algebra, usually studied in grade nine, is such a course. It contains a traditional package of algebraic concepts that students are supposed to understand and learn to use in a year of study. That year of study is carefully packaged in blocks of time known as Carnegie Units.

The Carnegie Unit was invented some eighty years ago to reduce confusion about the meaning of high school transcripts. Defined as classroom work with meetings four or five times a week over thirty-six weeks of the school year, it had the effect of freezing the way schools allocated time.[1] It also turned time spent in a class into a measure for promotion in grade and award of a diploma. Today students think of success in high school in terms of units completed rather than in terms of skills and understandings learned. This ancient, dead hand dominates our beliefs about learning achieved; it organizes secondary schools into time periods that are too short for effective learning; and it affects the planning of teachers and curriculum specialists for both what is taught and how it is taught. The only other places I know that measure success in terms of the time spent there are prisons and wine cellars.

137

TIME: THE PROCRUSTEAN BED

Let us look at the way our rigid use of time affects one course, first-year algebra. There is evidence that algebra, because of its high content of abstract thinking, is quite difficult for many students. Among eighth-graders choosing courses for the next year, it has a solid reputation as a tough course. Students do not want to take a course they might fail. So algebra becomes an anxiety builder to be avoided, and many students never take the first step on the academic path that leads to the numerous opportunities in modern life that require knowledge of science and mathematics.

The failure rate in beginning algebra is high enough to perpetuate the anxiety that can damage the future prospects of students. But evidence about the time factor in the study of algebra suggests a way out of this box. Back in the 1960s, when computers were first used in schools, the concept of "programmed learning" appeared as a potential use for these devices. Programmed learning involves a self-instructing process that provides basic information to the learner and then queries her about what she has learned. In a logically connected subject like algebra, it is possible to build a program that will lead students through the subject by giving them special help with elements they find difficult before going on to new topics.

With programmed learning, it turned out that some students could buzz through what was thought to be a year's work (one Carnegie Unit) very quickly, while others needed a much longer time and perhaps a different approach to get their minds around the intricacies of the subject. As explorations of this kind have increasingly demonstrated, the traditional allocation of time to courses is a real Procrustean bed. However, it is a factor that schools can do something about. Today quite a few schools are extending beginning algebra over a longer period of time, and they are also rethinking the way the subject is taught. By bringing situations from students' everyday lives to analyze in the classroom with algebraic tools, teachers are both motivating students and improving understanding.

In case I may be accused of advocating programmed instruction as a cheap way to run schools without teachers, let me plead not guilty. Programmed learning is a potential tool to augment the learning that is planned and encouraged by teachers, not a prescription for teachers' replacement—a generalization that applies to most technological applications to schooling. Much of what is done in schools does not lend itself to self-instruction alone. This is particularly true in realms of learning that spring from the humanities. Some wag has made an incisive comment about the relationship of the humanities to programmed instruction, in the form of a limerick:

The word has come down from the Dean
That by using a teaching machine,
Oedipus Rex could have learned about sex
Without ever disturbing the Queen.[2]

As for the types of learning that we want students to acquire in school, they are all improved for learners by the personal presence of teachers, who at their best both motivate inquiry by their questions and encourage performance by rewarding student progress with human warmth. Machines aren't good at that.

We build pressure based on time into the systems we use

to measure students' achievement. The tests we give almost always require that the questions be answered in a limited period of time. Indeed, the high muck-a-mucks of psychometrics regard time limits as a legitimate aspect of testing to help sort out the good students from those with more limited talents. But if a kid can answer more test questions in additional time, why not let him do it? This aspect of tests has always worried me. I'd like to know, for example, what proportion of students would do better on the SAT if they had more time to work on it and were, therefore, under less pressure. Of course, there are practical problems with such ideas. If more time were allowed, the test-takers would have to break for lunch, creating complexities in test administration and test security, not to mention the issue of who would provide the lunch. When we start treating students as people, schooling gets complicated.

My favorite story about testing gives a hint about the importance of time. In the 1860s at Hampton Institute (now Hampton University) in Virginia, an institution founded to offer education to the recently freed slaves, a former slave showed up seeking admission. As a test, the woman who was the academic principal of the Institute asked him to clean a room that was both dirty and disorderly.* He spent several hours at the task, much longer than expected. When he reported to her that the job was done, she put on white gloves and checked every corner for cleanliness. He had done a perfect job and was admitted.

---

* This would not have been the usual test for admission, of course, but a spur-of-the-moment decision on the principal's part.

After he graduated and after several years of further experience, this man went to Alabama and founded another institution for blacks, Tuskegee Institute. His name was Booker T. Washington. Sometimes I wonder whether Hampton would have admitted him if he had been given only one hour to clean the room.

The rigid pacing of learning in institutions doesn't stop with elementary and secondary schools. It goes on into colleges and universities, where the semester hour takes the place of the Carnegie Unit and where it is strongly believed that four academic years or their equivalent in part-time studies are needed for a college degree, no matter what the student is like or what his or her learning objectives may be. This temporal rigidity is possibly even more irrational in higher education than in schools, because by the time they enter college students have even more diversity of learning and learning skills among them. The belief in eight semesters with four courses in each for a bachelor's degree is a sanctified principle that has more to do with preserving institutions and their academic departments than with serving the learning needs of students. Also, it takes about three years to develop a really good blocking back on a football team. Come to think of it, athletic coaches could teach the academic faculty a thing or two. If they get a student with talent, they put him on the varsity team right away without making him go through lower-level teams first. They ask "What can he do?" rather than "How long has he prepared?"

Before I go on to some other sins committed by education in the name of time, let me correct any impression that I believe in accelerating children and youth in school and in making their level of learning the sole determinant of where they are placed in classes. The issue is not that simple. To deal with it, we have to go back to the psychologists, who made an appearance in Chapter 6. If there were a workable and reliable way to determine a youngster's developmental age, that would be the best single basis for organizing young people into groups, at least up through early adolescence, say to age fourteen or fifteen. But there isn't any such instrument short of getting each student into clinical treatment. Generally speaking, in these early years schools would be more effective if operated on the basis of age with flexibility for individuals, particularly in the K-3 years, when such flexibility is relatively easy to organize. Theoretically it works as well in a purely academic sense in later years, but then social cross-currents make it more problematic. An able sixth grader may belong in advanced placement mathematics, but may well feel like a fish out of water at the junior prom.

There is some evidence that mixing age groups on the basis of academic performance can work socially as well. Shortly after World War II an exploration of alternatives for able high school students took place. At the end of the sophomore year of high school, a number of carefully selected students were admitted to four universities: Columbia, Chicago, Wisconsin, and Yale. The program had served 1,350 students by 1950; eight other colleges joined it in 1951. Many thoughtful teachers and principals expressed concern that these young men and women might find the social and personal aspects of colleges a daunting experience for which they were unready. It didn't work out that way. They did well on all fronts, socially as well as academically.[3]

At the same time there was extensive exploration of an

alternative strategy, teaching college-level courses in high school instead of admitting students to college early. This strategy, launched by the College Board in the mid-1950s and known as the Advanced Placement Program, has come to be the dominant form of acceleration in secondary school. In the high school class that graduated in June of 1992, 378,000 students had taken one or more courses in high school that brought them college credit as freshmen. Often this college credit gives students who have a deep interest in a particular field the chance for more advanced work in the early years of higher education. In addition to Advanced Placement courses and their verifying examinations, there have been numerous special arrangements between particular schools and colleges to combine their programs to fit the learning needs of their students. Although most of these programs, such as Minnesota's voucher program for study in college by high school students, move students upward, there are also examples of high schools serving college students with special learning needs.

Tracking

In spite of these admirable examples of flexibility, most schools are still dominated by rigid ways of thinking about time. My main complaint about this rigidity concerns the way it leads us to think about and treat students. By far the most common response to the constraints imposed by the traditional time structure of schooling is *tracking*, a practice based on the concept that students are more teachable when they are grouped together on the basis of their academic achievement. The unwritten logic goes like this: "Because we have to teach these slower-learning kids in the same amount of time as those fast-learning kids, the way to avoid failure for the slow ones is to give them a less demanding curriculum." This logic automatically imposes lower expectations in the classroom for students in the lower tracks. When all the students in a class are low performers, the easiest and perhaps the most understandable assumption by the teacher is that they cannot perform at the level other students do. So their curriculum is diluted, and limitations are placed on their achievement early in their school years in a manner that becomes self-perpetuating.

Tracking is almost universally practiced in secondary schools and also appears widely in elementary schools through an emphasis on within-class groupings—the bumblebees, the squirrels, and the butterflies. And the opinion of most American teachers is strongly on the side of this practice: many teachers believe that homogeneous grouping is both desirable and necessary for successful learning. Extensive analysis of classroom situations, however, has shown that many youngsters are damaged by tracking, and further that heterogeneous classes, when properly taught, can work better for both slow learners and fast learners.[4]

In my judgment, the current debate among educators about the practice of tracking is the most important within-the-school issue we face—much more important than school choice, perhaps more important than school financing, clearly more important than the use of technology in schools, although that may be useful in breaking up the practice of tracking because it can help to individualize learning. Tracking is one of the most destructive aspects of factory-model schooling. It makes school a mediocre experience for too many students. In a society as socially and economically diverse as ours, tracking turns schools into organizations that could not be better designed to perpetuate disadvantage. Because it often tends to group students from privileged backgrounds separately from those from disadvantaged backgrounds, it fosters racial and cultural isolation and encourages low expectations for black and Hispanic students. It often creates islands of color or culture inside a school that reinforce the segregating influences outside the school. What is more, its overwhelming support from teachers and other educators makes it a difficult policy for our schools to change.

The time factor is only one of the reasons given for tracking in schools, but it is an important one. Uncritical acceptance of long-established patterns prevents us from trying new arrangements that might produce more success if teachers were willing to take on the challenge of change. One such change would be to provide more time for slower learners; another would be to vary what teachers and students do in the learning process. In photography, if you change the intensity of the light and the length of the exposure in the right ways, you will get a better picture. Making similar adjustments in a classroom will have the same effect on learning.

At the same time we need to recognize that a valuable program like Advanced Placement depends in part on the selection of students capable of doing the work required in the time allowed for it. And at the other end of the learning spectrum, special education, some individual needs are clearly difficult to meet in regular heterogeneous classes. So some elements of tracking are beneficial. To move toward a system of school organization in which tracking will not be a basic element we will have to make fundamental changes both in the use of time and in pedagogy.

The Fragmented School Day

Our rigid attitudes toward time also affect the way we divide up the time students and teachers spend together. Although most elementary schools retain an element of flexibility through the tradition of a single teacher for each class in a grade, that flexibility is increasingly impinged upon as specific time is reserved for studying music or art or science or math, often with special teachers who come into the classroom at scheduled times. So the trip to a local marsh that may be central to learning related to both environmental issues and biological science is hard to schedule because of time conflicts.

High schools and also many junior highs are trapped in a time bind related to the Carnegie Unit. High schools maintain an unwritten but powerful treaty among the major academic departments; it requires that every major course will have the same amount of time (with the exception of laboratory-based courses, which sometimes get more). Typically, classes meet for forty to fifty minutes four or five times a week; the day is divided into a homeroom period to begin with, a lunch time of thirty minutes or so, and about seven class periods. Five-minute breaks between classes use up half an hour of each day. Students without a class in a particular period go to study hall or the library but are generally restricted to independent study rather than learning activities with other students or teachers.

In a contest for the school schedule that would be most

useful for inhibiting learning and preventing imaginative teaching, the schedule in most high schools today would get first prize. Consider some of the handicaps this common arrangement of time creates: Any in-depth class discussion of a significant topic is almost certain to be cut short by the bell for the next class. Any effort to have groups of students work together to fashion a report on an issue is handicapped by being split into several class sessions, so that understandings reached in one session have to be reestablished at the next. Any activity that takes students outside the school is impossible without interrupting another class. Teachers typically have little or no chance to work together to change and improve courses; if a teacher has a free period, both the teachers and the students she might want to talk with are trapped in other classes. The short class sessions have a frenetic quality as attendance must be taken, homework checked on, a new assignment announced and clarified, and then learning promoted in some fashion that includes all students and advances the course of study. This chopped-up division of time in high schools has much to do with John Goodlad's judgment that many classes are dull because the teacher does almost all the talking. The allocation of time traps the teachers into such behavior.

Promising Proposals

So far the school reform movement has shown an interest in two different aspects of change in the use of time. The first of these was stirred up by one of the sensible proposals in *A Nation at Risk*: the recommendation to extend the school year. In the United States, usually by state law or regulation, schools are required to be open at least 180 days a year or a few more, and actual instructional time runs at about six to six and one-half hours a day. These state laws go way back, to the time when many Americans farmed and local school districts had a way of closing schools when young people were needed for farm work. In effect, the states were standing up for educational standards when they required at least 180 days of school. But they kept the number low to keep the farmers happy. Nowadays, about three percent of Americans work on farms, and machinery does much of what kids once did. Furthermore, many of the countries we see as our competitors in the world market-place have longer school years than we do.

Some U.S. cities have extended the school year by using the summer, but mainly for catch-up work for students who aren't doing well. Some have also made room for more kids in the schools by having some regular classes in the summer as part of the required 180 days. This is the way that Dartmouth College, under President John Kemeney, made room when it began to accept women students. Dartmouth started a regular semester in the summer and required all students to choose it at least once in their four years of college, thus creating dormitory space during the rest of the year. It reminds me of the U.S. Navy's practice of having sailors who had been on watch sleep in the bunks of those who relieved them, a system known as "hot sacking it." A label Dartmouth might prefer to avoid.

This kind of shift, however, does not extend the length of a student's education. The student just attends at a different time when there is space, thus promoting efficiency in the use of buildings. The big problem with really extending the time of schooling is that it costs a pot of money. If teachers are asked to serve an additional twenty working days a year, they quite reasonably want an added month's salary and related benefits. Financing of American schools is in such disarray that I see little possibility of extensive change in the annual calendar. Anyway, it doesn't make much sense to extend the year if schools continue to use time so poorly in their daily routines. More of what we now have in the factory model of schooling is not worth the cost.

The factory model is being challenged, as least in a few places, by some very imaginative changes in the daily schedules of schools. Those changes take a variety of formats, of which I will mention only a few. In the schools stimulated by Ted Sizer's thinking and in quite a number of others as well, the rigid and brief daily class meetings are being replaced by classes two periods or more long. This change challenges teachers to rethink what they and students do in a class. The change may be accomplished by bringing several subjects together: a teacher may work with a normal-sized class for two double periods a week while integrating their work in English and social studies or perhaps in mathematics and science. More can be accomplished in two double periods than in five single ones, and the teacher will have only two such classes, cutting the student load in half and offering added time for student conferences or work with other teachers. Having each teacher work with a smaller number of students encourages both more contact with parents and the assignment of more student writing.

TIME: THE PROCRUSTEAN BED

The most radical proposal I have seen for rearranging time and the other elements of schooling comes from Joseph M. Carroll. In Los Alamos, New Mexico, in the 1960s, Carroll launched a summer program, not for remediation but for added learning opportunities for all students who wanted to take it. He found that students could learn as much or more through intensive study of a single high school subject (chemistry, math, English, or history) for four hours a day, five days a week for six weeks as in the traditional forty-five minutes daily for 180 days. He also found that teachers and students liked the intensive study more than the usual arrangement.

This experience with restructuring the school schedule was a starting point for Carroll's later formulation of what he calls the Copernican Plan for secondary schools. He proposes that each student enroll in only one course at a time, meeting four hours each day for thirty days. Six of these courses would constitute a year's work. He argues that the varied teaching and learning techniques that become feasible in this more flexible time pattern, including a major growth of individualized instruction, can be much more successful than present high school practice. Together with the concentrated learning experiences in major fields of study, he advocates a daily interest/issue seminar of about seventy minutes based on broad topics and bringing together the skills and information from the several disciplines studied in the four-hour classes. These seminars might have a variety of forms and focuses, from environmental issues, to student work in community service, to major experiences in the arts and music.

It is easy to think of practical difficulties such a program would confront: a student sick with the flu for a week would miss the entire Civil War in history class; in a foreign language isn't continuity of use important along with intensive exposure? Perhaps adjustments would have to be made to the plan to get around such problems. At the very least, however, I find Carroll's conception a useful guide to rethinking the ways we use time in schools. And readers of his essay on the Copernican Plan will find that he has foreseen most of the difficulties inherent in his plan.[5]

Another issue in secondary schools is how much time teachers and students should spend together in the typical class situation. Shouldn't students as they get older be encouraged to play a growing role in their own education? I still recall the feeling of satisfaction I had in my senior year of secondary school when my English teacher excused me from the regular English class and let me take a full semester to read the plays of Euripides, Sophocles, Aeschylus, and Aristophanes. I worked much harder than I would have in the class, and I met occasionally and informally with the teacher and several other students working on the same arrangement. We felt we were being trusted as adults, and we responded accordingly. Opportunities for independent work in high school prepare students well for college, but the opportunities won't come their way unless the time schedules of both students and teachers are loosened.

All these ideas for change are worth pursuing and are promising signs that we may overcome the rigidity that turns the use of time in schools into a Procrustean bed. It is vital to recognize, however, that absolutely nothing can be accomplished by having the President of the United States or the Secretary of Education or the Congress or chief state school officers or state legislatures or school boards or school superintendents or school principals cast themselves in the role of Theseus and decide to legislate or direct or otherwise impose by fiat these revisions in educational practices. Any progress has to be accomplished by creating a situation in which teachers want to take the risk of getting out of their ruts and seeking new strategies both individually and collectively. When teachers are ready to move, then the assignment for all these parties that want to improve schools from outside the classroom should be to support teachers in the place where the essential action happens.

8

Classrooms, Teachers, and Principals

Automobile advertising has come up with the phrase "where the rubber meets the road" as an expression of the essence of all that is significant about the capacity of a motor car to perform. In schools, the place where the rubber meets the road is the classroom. As Edward Pauly puts it in his book *The Classroom Crucible*, "the success or failure of the school depends on daily life in classrooms."[1] This truth, as Pauly also points out, is often overlooked by those who seek to reform our schools.

Most of what happens in the daily life of classrooms is shaped by teachers and principals. Just as I have argued that schools need to recognize that students are people, I intend to argue here for more attention to that same simple generalization as it applies to the classroom and the adults within it and responsible for it. Both teachers and principals work in demanding jobs characterized by endless pressures that sometimes cause burnout. Both must interact all day long with other human beings for whom or to whom they carry responsibility. Both are tempted to avoid any personal involvement with the students or teachers for whom they are responsible, and both know that unless they establish such relationships, their work runs the risk of failure. Both are continually challenged to seek ways to do their jobs better, and both are employees of the local board of education, which typically shows only limited interest in providing the seed money to help them improve what they do. Together with parents they carry on their shoulders the most weighty responsibility of any group of Americans—ensuring that the next generation will mature into adults capable of advancing the causes of humanity and decency in an increasingly complex world.

The established patterns in schools often keep these hardworking educators isolated and without support. Deborah Meier, the principal of Central Park East Secondary School in New York City, has written incisively about the tendency of schools to ignore the human characteristics of professional educators:

> Human beings by nature are social, interactive learners. We check out our ideas, argue with authors, bounce issues back and forth, ask friends to read our early drafts, talk together after seeing a movie, pass on books we have loved, attend meetings and argue our ideas, share stories and gossip that extends our understanding of ourselves and others. Talk lies at the heart of our lives. This kind of exchange is never allowed in school, nor modeled there—not between children, nor between adults. . . .
>
> If we intend dramatically to improve education of Amer-

ican children, we need to invent very different environments for them. Teachers must be challenged to invent schools they would like to teach in organized around the principles of learning that we know matter.[2]

Wherever one looks today among the most thoughtful analysts of American school practice, the centerpiece of change is this general principle of making the classroom a stimulating, friendly, and purposeful place characterized by the active participation of everyone in it—a place where both students and teachers want to be. John Goodlad's intensive study of a cross-section of American schools comes to that conclusion. James Comer's orchestration of the human relationships of the school plays the same tune. Theodore Sizer's definition of the teacher as coach to encourage and guide learning activities carried out by students also fits neatly under this rubric.

What seems to me to have happened in the so-called school reform movement since the early '80s resembles the pattern of thesis, antithesis, and synthesis found in Hegelian philosophy. The commission that issued *A Nation at Risk* first dominated thinking about our schools with an exaggerated condemnation calling for reform imposed from above; that blast of rhetoric was followed by a variety of critical analyses of both its accusations and its prescriptions, including the report of a commission that Marian Wright Edelman and I co-chaired: *Barriers to Excellence: Our Children at Risk.*[3] A synthesis has now emerged that recognizes the need for some top-down activity by the national government, state agencies, and local school boards. There is still a major debate raging about some aspects of the new synthesis, particularly the financing of schools, the value of choice as an element of school reform, and whether and by whom a national system of standards and assessments should be fashioned. But there is broad and general agreement that a major feature of school change for the future should be a shift toward more prerogatives for teachers, as well as for principals and parents, in defining what they do and how they do it.

"Restructuring" and "school-based management" (or "school-site management") are terms often heard in discussions of ways to decentralize school governance. There are no standard definitions of them as far as I know. Restructuring is a concept that came from the business world. As American companies experienced more international competition, they sought to cut their costs and make their organizations more efficient by decentralizing management. Instead of maintaining large central staffs to check up on subdivisions of the corporation, they gave the separate units more discretion about how to accomplish their tasks as long as objectives were met. This strategy allowed the mother company to unload a substantial number of costly middle-management people. In addition, it allowed the local units to tap the imagination and creativity of their employees, whose task formerly had been to do what the central office ordered. In a number of major corporations this model of restructuring was quite successful in improving competitive performance.

Business executives interested in the schools helped to transplant the general concept of restructuring to both state-wide and local school systems. Large and expensive bureaucracies in cities have become targets of this change in thinking, as a number of cities have moved toward giving more control to the individual school. In New York City, by the time he was let go by a narrow-minded school board, Joe Fernandez had begun to whittle away the city's mammoth bureaucracy. In Chicago, special state legislation has given each school in the system more power to control its own affairs through a new system of governance under which parents, teachers, and the principal work together in a School Council empowered to make many decisions about personnel, curriculum, organization, and pedagogy. Cincinnati, in September 1992, announced a major reduction in middle management that would save millions of dollars—money that could be made available for direct support of instruction in the schools.

Whatever term is used to describe it, the move toward decentralization has caught on and is being pursued in many school systems, each with its own bells and whistles. It usually carries two concepts: freedom of invention to meet the needs of the children in the particular school, and the responsibility to perform reasonably well in an assessment process required by the school board and superintendent. (To some extent, this move toward more freedom for schools is threatened by the simultaneous demand for national standards and tests, which I will address in the next chapter.)

In the wave of enthusiasm for decentralization of school governance, it is important to realize that a mere change of governance is not enough. Giving a school some flexible funds and allowing it to decide how to use them can create a heady situation for a new governing council with parents and teachers as members. But the council may end up bickering for hours over whether to refurbish the playground or improve the library or a little bit of both. And whatever it decides on this kind of issue will not make a major change in the school. If any really useful change is to be accomplished by a change in governance, an effort must be made to answer two important questions and deal with their implications: (1) What changes should we make here to serve our students better? and (2) What is required to make this school a better workplace for teachers? A careful effort to answer these two questions will come up with problems or needs that point to specific changes that should be assigned a high priority. If a school can agree on such items it can then make a plan to do something about them.

Enlisting Teachers for Change

This emphasis on change from the bottom up—on giving teachers more control of schools and particularly of what happens in their classrooms—seems to me the most promising strategy so far offered for improving the country's schools. Having said that, however, I must quickly add that such change is extremely difficult to bring about. Susan Moore Johnson underlines this problem:

> There is no certainty that changes in practice follow changes in policy. Deciding that a school district should embark on school site management is only the first step in a long process that requires many other changes to achieve decentralization—reorienting hierarchical relationships between central offices and schools, developing new decision-making skills among teachers and parents who are unpracticed in school governance, preparing principals and teachers for new kinds of leadership at the school site.[4]

None of these promising changes can come about without the support of teachers. Whatever the policy, no amount of "legislated learning" will improve the schools unless the teachers are for it. Until recently the school reform movement largely ignored teachers, with the one exception that *A Nation at Risk* strongly advocated merit pay for teachers on the theory that the offer of more money would persuade them to shape up and do a good job. This hoary suggestion with a long record of failure in numerous trials over the years was an insult to teachers, who found themselves unappreciated, beleaguered by large classes, unsupplied with classroom materials, harassed by bureaucratic routines, and unconsulted about the changes in schools that were being demanded. If teachers are to be enlisted to support school reform, their feelings based on these circumstances must be kept in mind. They act as other people would when subjected to a confusing combination of neglect and harassment by outsiders with limited understanding of their classroom trials and tribulations.

One might think that a proposal to give teachers more control in the classroom would automatically be a hit with teachers. However, as Deborah Meier has pointed out, because of "the constraints of the job plus old habits and a kind of societal nostalgia for what school 'used to be like,'" teachers are often "part of the broader inertia that makes fundamental change hard to implement." Policymakers who want to improve the quality of schooling, Meier says, must "change the conditions of teaching. They must offer incentives for change and above all the resources (in this case the key is well-designed staff development time) to enable teachers to learn from their changed conditions."[5]

And even attempts to overcome teachers' part of this "broader inertia" must be shaped by input from teachers. A high school history teacher interviewed by Edward Pauly expressed some skepticism about the new emphasis on decentralization:

> Policies that take classrooms seriously would be a whole new way of looking at the way schools work. Some of the talk about reform now is about this school-based management stuff, but still, it's *school*-based management; it's all based on the idea that we've just got to get a principal we can trust, and he can control all those lousy teachers. So they're still a step away from the classroom . . . I think they don't *care* what's going on in the classrooms, as long as they don't hear it in the halls. So you would have to change the power structure so that the teachers and the students were the ones who were able to shape what was going on.[6]

Classrooms for Active Learning

With this background on the inherent difficulties of bottom-up change, let's look at some examples of classroom practice that require rethinking by teachers and principals in schools. The most pernicious aspect of the factory model of schooling still reflected in our classrooms is the dominance of the teacher's voice in all activities. Students sit passively in neat rows and listen while teachers talk. Student-to-student communication is occasional or banned. Working together by students in small groups claims little classroom time, partly because class periods are too short and partly because teachers have no time for the careful planning such activities require of them. Frequent tests are given and students get grades that tell them how they are doing, but teachers also have very limited opportunities for giving special help to youngsters who have not mastered the material. A concept of coverage dominates the learning process, and when a unit of work is completed and students have been tested on it, the class rolls forward to a new topic even though some members don't really understand what has just been "covered." The assumption is that students who don't get it may have to fail and repeat the year.

All of this adds up to an assembly-line process that is imposed from above and sustained by required testing and required curriculum coverage. It is a process in which students come rapidly to believe that education is something that is done to you, not an endeavor in which you as a person are engaged along with a teacher who is helping you to educate yourself. Although very capable teachers can find ways within this regimen to make classes interesting and to help students who don't understand the day's work, the adjustments made to introduce those elements into the steamroller of routines that dominates most classrooms are very demanding of teachers.

The nature of the factory model of schooling leads most teachers to be supporters of tracking, in which the most successful students are grouped together and the least successful get the same treatment. My views on tracking should be clear from the previous chapter: I consider it the deepest rut in which the factory model mires our schools. And I am not alone; a growing body of research shows that heterogeneous grouping is preferable for both low-achieving and high-achieving students. But I do not believe we should simply abolish the practice—not without very careful planning, planning carried out within the schools where the change will take place and with participation by the teachers who will be involved. As I have noted, most teachers believe in tracking. Susan Moore Johnson analyzed the views of 115 very able teachers and found that they supported homogeneous rather than heterogeneous grouping for instruction.[7] A number of them thought that reduction of tracking was desirable but would require smaller classes than their school system allowed—a major item of expense. Those of us who are pushing for the detracking of schools must keep in mind that it will require major help for teachers to adjust to new classroom practices, efforts to explain to parents why such changes should take place, and reexamination of numerous familiar internal practices in schools.

The *Harvard Education Letter*'s overview of the recent literature on tracking opens with a quotation from John D'Auria, a middle school principal in Wellesley, Massachusetts: "If tracking would help us accomplish our goals at this school, then we would use it. But we believe in producing active learners, critical thinkers, and risk takers, and tracking every student by ability quite simply doesn't allow us to achieve our goals."[8] The use of the phrase "active learners" as a contrast to what tracking would produce brings us back to the promising initiatives that are being designed to turn students into active seekers of learning and classrooms into stimulating places to be.

What does D'Auria mean by "producing active learners"? I have to guess because I haven't asked him, but I am fairly sure that he has in mind classroom routines that encourage students to work together to explore information and ideas that will help them to understand a situation or to solve a problem. I remember an example from my days as a junior high school principal in the 1950s. A group of eighth graders studied a proposal to add fluoride to the local drinking water for the prevention of tooth decay. At the time this now universal practice was controversial. Some citizens considered fluoride a poison, which indeed it is if you drink enough of it. Others were against the proposal on ideological grounds, believing that putting fluoride in the public water supply was tantamount to imposing national health care by government fiat. A religious group with some political strength in the community saw fluoridation as contrary to its beliefs. The local selectmen were split on the issue, and they were annoyed that the eighth graders were investigating it. These kids learned a great deal about science, about local politics, about how difficult and irrational adults can be, and about their own power to investigate real issues and learn from doing so. This last item was probably their most important lesson.

Good teachers, of course, have been stirring up such learning opportunities for years. The Foxfire enterprise launched many years ago by Eliot Wigginton in Rabun Gap, Georgia, is wonderful proof that high school students can reach genuine depth in their learning by writing and publishing about the past in their own communities. Anyone who has heard Wigginton and his teenaged colleagues explain how they operate understands the concept of active learning.[9] Active learning can infiltrate any subject area— even mathematics. Algebra students in New York City are learning to use algebraic concepts from their schools in analyzing certain aspects of the subway system, and in doing so they see more sense in studying algebra than they did before.

Another example from my own experience comes from the North Carolina Advancement School, an institution launched in Winston Salem in 1964. At that time I was working on rethinking schools in the state for Governor Terry Sanford, who had a major interest in improving them. We set up the Advancement School to serve eighth-grade boys whose academic records suggested that they might soon become dropouts. Attendance was voluntary for a six-month period of intensive academic and motivational stimulation, much of it in the form of active learning. When the school faculty and its principal, Gordon McAndrew, asked themselves "What are eighth-grade boys most interested in?" the answer was simple: "Sex and automobiles." They figured the new school might be criticized for focusing its science and math programs on sex, so they went to used-car dealers and collected some of their cast-offs for teaching these subjects. With a little imagination the automobile can be used as a base for many areas of learning, and both students and faculty found the venture exciting. There was evidence that the school reduced dropping out among those who attended it.

Despite such examples of successful experiments with active learning, the concept has not yet taken hold in most of our nation's schools. Kim Marshall, an elementary school principal in Boston, paints a vivid picture of how far the typical factory-model classroom routine is from the promotion of active learning:

> Effective teachers know that active, hands-on experiences teach best. An ancient Chinese proverb says:

CLASSROOMS, TEACHERS, AND PRINCIPALS

Tell me and I forget.
Show me and I remember.
Involve me and I understand.

Yet all too many classrooms are a passive experience for all but a few eager, hand-waving students who know the answers. Even in many classrooms considered exemplary, the teacher is performing and perspiring at the front of the room and students are doing precious little thinking, talking, and writing. The question might well be asked, *Who's doing the work here?* In such classrooms, the teacher has become an entertainer, a surrogate TV set. The tragedy is that this kind of classroom satisfies almost everyone: the teacher feels he or she is working hard; the students are entertained; administrators see a quiet, "engaged" class; and parents believe that this teacher-centered format is the way it is supposed to be—it worked for them, so why not for their kids?[10]

How are we to make the transition from classrooms in which teachers act as "surrogate TV sets" to classrooms in which students, with coaching from teachers, actively pursue their own learning? As my earlier quotation from Deborah Meier testified, the most essential need of teachers and principals if they are to make changes in classroom procedures is free time to explore possibilities, to make plans, to try out new teaching and learning projects, and to discuss with colleagues how the new ideas are working and how they can be improved. What our schools need now is the kind of daily planning time and collegial work that has long been part of teachers' regular routine in a number of Asian countries. Various strategies might be used to meet this need for staff development time: reorganizing the school day, as discussed in Chapter 7, to give all teachers more flexible time than they now have; providing funds for substitutes to shake key teachers loose for staff development planning; arranging for additional days during the year when teachers can work together; using vacation and summer breaks to employ teachers for work on staff development.

Nowadays, as both school districts and states operate under strong budget pressures, there is an unfortunate tendency to cut staff development funds as a low-priority item. The political pressure for these cuts, which frequently make only a few people lose their jobs, is very strong. It's a practice that resembles eating your seed corn—it keeps people from being hurt in the short term but creates disaster in the future. It would make good sense for school boards wrestling with restructuring efforts to commit any funds saved by reducing administrative staff to the staff development function within individual schools.

Principals as Educators

Like everything else I am advocating for the schools, these suggestions for getting teachers to work together to change their classroom practice must be built on the willingness of teachers to take part. The school principal can do more than anyone else to promote that willingness. This suggests that what can be accomplished in a school depends on the human relationships that the principal forges with teachers—and this suggestion raises a bevy of questions. How do we prepare and select school principals? How are their responsibilities best defined? How can they be helped to become more effective? Is there any such thing as truly effective training in school leadership?

Although graduate schools of education, such as the one I work in at Harvard, can offer courses to arm both practicing and potential principals with useful information and ideas, their capacity to inculcate the many sensitivities a principal must have to succeed in improving what happens in classrooms is limited. And there are so many cross-currents today about requirements for the principalship that it is difficult for a school of education to know where to start. Some see the principal's role as a management position and urge preparation similar to that offered in business schools. This concept has been carried so far that there are strong advocates for recruiting school principals from management jobs in the business world.

I believe strongly that the odds are against success for any person in the principalship who has not been a successful teacher. I do not believe that effective school principals can be trained in university classrooms; instead, they have to be grown in schools. These beliefs are based on the assumption that the central role of the principal is primarily one of helping teachers to find ways to make classrooms work better. When that is the task to be accomplished, the subtleties of relationships with teachers, students, and parents become the keys to success.

None of these views of mine should be taken as opposing experimentation with school leadership. There are schools where experienced teachers take turns being principal, other schools that divide up the principal's role in various ways. Why not, for example, have an academic principal and a lower-paid manager to oversee the building, the lunch-room, and the business aspects of the school?

Originally the word "principal" was used simply to designate the teacher in the school who was in charge. In small schools the "principal-teacher" was also a full-time teacher. In today's larger and more complex schools, the principal usually no longer teaches in the traditional sense, although there are interesting examples of returning to the old principal-teacher arrangement. Unless the person in the principal's job becomes a teacher and a helper of teachers rather than a manager for students, parents, and teachers, the school won't work as well as it might. A truly effective teacher is one who believes every pupil can learn, who has in-depth knowledge of what is to be learned, who is resourceful about finding learning strategies that work for students who have difficulties, who is acutely aware of the need for home support of school learning and gives time and effort to arranging it, and who knows the difference between active and passive learning and reaches always for the former. Principals who are genuinely committed to these purposes will spread them throughout their schools, and they will do this with confidence because they learned how in their own experience as teachers.

Schools lucky enough to have such a principal will find that discipline and control, so often seen as the defining strengths of school principals by the boards of education that appoint them, are much less important than is commonly believed. When superintendents and boards of education learn to see principals primarily as educators rather than managers and disciplinarians, the "classroom crucible" will foster a schoolwide atmosphere in which there will be fewer behavior problems because the students will be generally interested in what's afoot in classrooms. In addition, this perception of the principal's role will mean that many more school principals will be women. Today about 70 percent of teachers are women, but the percentages of female principals in elementary and secondary schools are about 20 and 12 respectively, and only 4 percent of school superintendents are women. The stereotype of the school principal as a former physical education teacher and coach who can "handle" the tough kids is dying too slowly. It was recently revived by a bully with a bullhorn from New Jersey, who made headlines across the country and now makes money as an education consultant.

Principals must have some authority because they have responsibility for the safety and the educational success of both teachers and students. The nature of authority is elusive. It is an element of association with other people that is most effective when it is not used, a paradox that successful principals understand. If you force someone to do something instead of creating a situation that will make him or her want to do it, you have won the battle and lost the war. This is a truth about the roles of all leaders in all kinds of organizations.

The relationships principals build with the teachers in their schools must be based on mutual trust. Building such relationships takes time, diplomacy, and a genuine quality of caring for teachers and respecting their work. Earlier I spoke of the importance of finding time in the routines of a school for teachers to think about their work and to reflect with colleagues about what is working in their classrooms and what isn't. For teachers, their teaching is the work that gives their lives meaning, and dissecting it alone is hard enough; doing so with others may be truly threatening. An atmosphere of trust is important to encourage honest self-assessment and willingness to experiment—qualities that are needed if our schools are to make the fundamental change from the assembly-line model to more humane and more constructive environments for learning. Even with such trust in the background, the hardest task principals have is telling a teacher that classroom performance is inadequate and must be changed for the better. Unless a principal can speak from experience in the classroom and can give specific suggestions for such a teacher to try, the message is likely to be destructive rather than supportive.

Besides supporting teachers, school principals need ways to foster their own growth in both performance and understanding as they suffer the daily battering of unexpected incidents that characterizes their job. Kim Marshall underlines the intensity of their work: "Principals have a constant deluge of activities vying for their attention . . . The action is relentless, and there is a constant struggle to keep one's own agenda in the forefront and use unexpected events to accomplish short- and long-term goals."[11] If teachers are willing to open their thinking and their classrooms to one another, they can reduce the isolation of their daily work and gain the advantages of colleagueship. But school principals have few such options. Their daily dose of small and large crises ranging from truancy to suicide goes on and on, and they have few opportunities to share insights with other principals.

The best innovation I have encountered to help principals gain perspective on their daily experiences is connected to the Harvard Graduate School of Education, but it is not controlled by the university. Called the Principals' Center at Harvard, it is a semi-independent organization with a governing board, and membership dominated by school principals. It raises a major portion of its budget through fees, grants, and special seminars to which principals come from all over the United States. It offers opportunities to principals for stimulating discussions about the rigors, rewards, and responsibilities of their profession. It encourages principals to write about their work, and it publishes their papers. When this organization was being formed in the early 1980s, the Boston school superintendent offered to pay for membership of all the city's principals if the Principals' Center would check up on their attendance. The governing board refused the offer. They wanted members who would participate voluntarily.

This model for professional growth is ideal. It treats its members as professionals; it trusts them to perceive and to plan for their own needs for stimulation and for letting off steam. It has been widely replicated in various ways around the country, and there is now a network of such organizations.

If we are to change what happens in classrooms from passive to active learning, we need a new style of leadership from principals and other educational leaders. Change in the classroom will occur only when teachers make up their minds to accept the challenge of such change. Teachers, in turn, will make that decision when they feel some confidence that there is support for such changes in the administrative and policy apparatus of school districts and states. For this to happen the hierarchy and bureaucracy we have created to operate and control our schools must change fundamentally. Both school superintendents and state commissioners of education, along with principals and other members of the administrative hierarchy, will have to define their roles as the enablers of classroom change determined by teachers—not as managers or policymakers who prescribe what teachers are to do.

This transformation of today's educational bosses into servants for teachers will be a slow game, and some of them may well fail to make the adjustment. The new-style leaders of education will define their own success as encouraging and stimulating the success of people for whose work they, as principals or superintendents or school boards or state commissioners of education, are responsible. They will build morale in the school and in the profession by contributing to the success of teachers in classrooms.

Attracting and Training Good Teachers

Despite their responsibility for helping the next generation mature into the kinds of adults our society needs, we hold educators at a relatively low status. This lack of status means that the profession may not be able to attract top-notch new recruits with the talent to do their jobs well.

There are various schools of thought about the best ways to attract talented people to these jobs. Some see a solution in removing bureaucratic certification requirements and letting liberal arts graduates with good college records into classrooms where, it is argued, they can master pedagogy relatively quickly. Others argue that schools of education should improve their training programs by building on the body of knowledge about the classroom and its complexities that has emerged from recent research on teaching.

I can't sort out these controversies in an orderly fashion, but I do have some comments on them. The first is that the place to learn to teach is in the classroom and not in the school of education, where much of the teaching that goes on has the same weaknesses that so many critics have found in the schools. Years ago, in an article entitled "Teaching and Tennis," I argued that learning to teach is like learning to play tennis. The only way you can do the latter is to get out on the tennis court with someone who is better at the game than you are. You can listen to lectures on tennis, watch movies of it, drink cocktails with expert players, and otherwise arrange contacts with the game. All these activities may well give you some ideas about tennis strategies, but they won't improve your serve, your forehand, or your backhand. Tennis must be mastered actively. So must teaching!

Like the schools themselves, our systems for preparing or improving teaching are too cluttered with passive learning and lacking in active learning. Many of our arrangements for practice teaching result in more observation than actual teaching. Aspiring teachers need more opportunities to plan a lesson, to teach it, and to get immediate feedback from one or more experienced teachers who have observed the classroom. Feedback from peers who are also preparing for teaching can be helpful, too—to both parties. The use of videotape can make the observation-and-feedback process more focused and more efficient.

Consider the active learning we require for the people

who will care for our children's bodies as compared with what we require for those who will care for the development of their minds. Prospective medical doctors spend several years as interns before we turn them loose to make their own judgments about the needs of their patients. A prospective teacher, in contrast, is likely to have practice teaching that is skimpy in the actual teaching time it offers and equally lacking in effective follow-up. And of course teachers also get much less basic scientific information about their future field of expertise, teaching and learning.

Dr. Everett Koop, a former Surgeon General of the United States and now dean of the Dartmouth Medical School, has launched an experiment in the preparation of M.D.s that offers educators a challenging model. Every student enrolled in Dartmouth Medical School, throughout the years of training, acts as a medical advisor to a nearby family with children. The student must establish a relationship, become a trusted advisor, and help both children and adults to understand their health and nutritional needs and problems. Why couldn't a school or department of education bring an element of reality to the preparation of teachers by establishing such an experience for all teachers in training— perhaps with two families, one with young children and the other with children of secondary school age?

Teacher preparation in this country also needs a major change in its internship arrangements. There should be more extensive internships as part of training, and it would make sense to have beginning teachers on their first job spend their first year as interns, with regular supervision from colleagues who are carefully chosen and well paid for the work involved. The compensation senior teachers get for the added burden of supervising an intern typically is below minimum wage or even nonexistent.

The Michigan Partnership for New Education is one initiative working to bring about fundamental change in all aspects of education, including the preparation of teachers. Supported in part by the Kellogg Foundation and led by Judith Lanier, this partnership has developed a comprehensive vision for educational change that, in the words of Thomas James, involves reconfiguring "not merely the classroom, not only the training of teachers, not just standards and testing, but a multiplicity of relationships among institutions and stakeholders that shape the educational process." James also states that if the Michigan Partnership "succeeds in becoming the driving force of educational change in the state of Michigan, every aspect of schooling must undergo self-renewal."[12]

The key to the potential of this major experiment—and to teachers' prospects of achieving full professional status—lies in the term "self-renewal." This phrase was given meaning and visibility by my old boss at the Department of Health, Education and Welfare, John W. Gardner, who wrote: "Unless we cope with the ways in which modern society oppresses the individual, we shall lose the creative spark that renews both society and men."[13] Although he might better have said "human beings" rather than "men," Gardner expressed a view that holds the key to changing our institutions—including schools—to meet the needs of the future. This magical concept of self-renewal can make the difference between imposed change characterized by reluctant foot-dragging and change from within that awakens enthusiasm and a sense of ownership that nourishes further commitment. These qualities of ownership and commitment have long been present in the service tradition of teaching. They are also major elements of professionalism. A profession is a calling that is based on a body of knowledge, that sets its own standards for performance, and that takes responsibility for staying abreast of the quality of its service to others. The regimentation of factory-model schooling is a barrier to professional status. To gain professional standing teachers must take more responsibility for their own self-renewal. One fortunate implication of the concept of *restructuring* is that it can open the door to self-renewal in schools.

A group contributing to the effort to gain professional status for teachers is the National Board for Professional Standards in Teaching (NBPST), a private nonprofit organization that was established in 1987 to launch a systematic approach to enhancing teachers' skills, knowledge, and classroom performance. NBPST is developing a comprehensive series of teacher assessments designed to lead to certification of teachers as skilled professionals. The assessments will not be limited to tests of subject-matter knowledge and academic understanding of child development and teaching skills; instead they will require teachers to demonstrate that they can use their knowledge effectively in classroom settings. Anyone with three years' experience teaching in a school, public or private, will be eligible to go through the assessment process in the hope of receiving certification of professional competence.

The board of directors of NBPST is largely made up of classroom teachers, thus imbuing this large-scale experiment with a valuable element of self-renewal. Other board members come from varied backgrounds—policymakers and politicians, school board members, union leaders, foundation staff members, and others. The NBPST president, James Kelly, has guided the organization with the same style of leadership needed to bring about change in schools—building on the success of colleagues in responding to new challenges.

Endeavors like the Michigan Partnership and NBPST are unusual in their focus on teachers; most proposals for school reform start with tests and standards rather than with teachers. The purveyors of new standards and new tests, if they don't give teachers a major role in changing schools, make three serious mistakes. They convey a lack confidence in teachers that is likely to inhibit improvement in classroom practice; they imply that their tests will be used to force teachers into accepting new standards, thus repeating a strategy that failed after the publication of *A Nation at Risk*; and they tend to ignore the upgrading of teacher preparation and school staff development that are essential for real change in classrooms.

As George Madaus of Boston University has pointed out, the governors who distilled the six National Education Goals did not even mention teachers. Madaus has a good idea for rectifying this omission—he suggests adding a seventh goal: "By the year 2000 America will have the best prepared, most highly respected teaching force in the world."[14]

To meet that goal by attracting highly talented people to the teaching profession, we will have to offer better pay than teachers get today. A few school districts in the country compensate teachers well. Most do not. The time when very able women would accept low-paying jobs in schools has gone by. Very able women now become lawyers, doctors, business executives, engineers, and the like. All the other countries whose schools we admire provide higher teaching salaries than we do, as well as higher social status for teachers. We are losing many of our best teachers to private business, particularly those in short supply—mathematics and science teachers.

The importance of this issue has been cogently described by Richard Murnane and several colleagues:

> Success in designing policies that attract skilled teachers to the nation's schools will affect the composition of the teaching force for years to come ... If [the new teachers] are primarily academically weak college graduates, who could find no more attractive jobs, the nation will pay the price for many years. If they are among the nation's academically talented graduates, and if they have learned the skills needed to teach effectively, the benefits will be long term indeed.[15]

If all the teachers in public schools were given a 50 percent salary increase next year, there would probably be very little change in school performance the following year—although the boost in morale might do some immediate good. But five years later the schools would be doing a better job, and the upward change would continue. Teachers' salaries are no different from other salaries in their capacity to raise performance by attracting better-prepared, more versatile, and more effective people. Teaching attracts some of its best people through its tradition of service, but the likelihood that that motive will guarantee an adequate supply of candidates with the combination of intellectual power, emotional balance, and capacity to grow on the job that is required of successful teachers is dim at best.

The basic aspect of school financing that ensures low salaries for too many teachers is the fact that about half the funds for schools are at risk in the decisionmaking of local taxpayers once a year. At a time when the preponderance of voters acting on school budgets is made up of oldsters with little interest in schools, members of America's growing cadre of childless people, and parents of private school students, the voices of support for adequate teachers' salaries are drowned out. There is a good chance that this tragic political imbalance, which is powerfully evident in many school districts from coast to coast, will undermine all the other initiatives that are beginning to appear for making schools more effective.

This chapter has had much more to say about classrooms than it has about schools. That emphasis is intentional. Those who view the individual school as the unit for educational change will be frustrated unless they pay serious attention to the individual classroom. The history of our schools in the twentieth century has been one of teachers in isolated classrooms—isolated in the sense of having little or no communication with other classrooms and teachers. Because, as Kim Marshall says, "teachers are without supervision 99 percent of the time,"[16] there is little assurance that defending the individual teacher in an isolated classroom is a workable strategy for change in schools. When the classroom door closes, the only obligation a teacher has is to cover the lesson for the day. As we have seen, that practice frequently results in an unconstructive learning process for students. What's needed is not more supervision of teachers. Instead, the key to improving both classrooms and schools is giving teachers time and opportunities for exchange with one another. Restructuring and school-site governance that do not reach to the fundamental level of the classroom are doomed to failure.

9

Saving the Nation with Tests and Standards?

I have argued that the decline of American schools supposedly revealed by SAT scores and international test comparisons has been unmercifully exaggerated. Although I am quite certain of that view, I am also enough of a realist to know when I have lost an argument. So I recognize that we are going to "fix" our schools. President Clinton wants to fix them (and so did his predecessor, George Bush), most governors do also, and a small army of business leaders, professors, educators, and editorial writers are converts to the belief that American schools were once good but have turned bad.

While I am not against fixing the schools (I would prefer to say "helping the schools fix themselves"), my assessment of what's wrong and how to fix it differs from that of many of today's leaders of education. They diagnose the patient as having recently come down with a severe disease and needing intensive care by specialists, strong antibiotics, and frequent tests to monitor progress. My diagnosis is a persistent low-level ailment that doesn't keep the patient from working but does detract from the quality of the work. The patient's nutrition and work environment both contribute to this condition, and both must be changed to restore health. Unlike those who believe only drastic remedies prescribed from above will do the trick, I am convinced that the patient, with some help, can accomplish much of the healing from within.

The Economy Again

Not only do the worthy leaders of education agree about the illness of the schools; they are also convinced that the decline of the schools is responsible for the decline of the economy. American corporations are said to be having a tough time competing in international markets because of an undereducated work force. I am an educator and not an economist, but I suspect that the responsibility of the schools for what is wrong with the economy is another thing that has been seriously exaggerated.

I showed in Chapter 1 that much of the decline in average SAT scores over the years resulted from a proud record of bringing new segments of the population into the college-going stream, many of them from impoverished communities and schools that were inadequate for college preparation. While this was a signal calling for special attention to such schools and to the living conditions of poor children, it was not evidence of across-the-board failure of American schools.

There is plenty of other evidence that our schools have been doing something right. For example, between 1978 and 1991 the number of students taking Advanced Placement tests to gain college credit for high school work expanded from 90,000 to 324,000. Asians tripled their participation in Advanced Placement; African Americans doubled theirs; and Hispanics quadrupled theirs. In the same period, African Americans, Asians, Native Americans, Mexican Americans, and Puerto Ricans increased their average scores on the SAT substantially. High school graduation rates increased from about 60 percent of an age cohort in 1960 to 75 percent in 1975. The National Assessment of Educational Progress, based upon a national sample of nine-, thirteen-, and seventeen-year-olds in mathematics, science, reading, writing, geography, and computer skills, has shown slow but steady gains since the early 1970s. And standardized tests used regularly by many schools—the California Achievement Tests, the Iowa Test of Basic Skills, the Stanford Achievement Test, the Metropolitan Achievement Test, and the Comprehensive Test of Basic Skills—showed regular gains in learning in both reading and mathematics in the 1970s and 1980s.[1] Thus the negative effects on the competitive prospects of American business were not caused by the decline of test-measurable learning in the schools.

It seems to me much more likely that America's troubles with competitiveness stem from other sources, ranging from shortsighted business management to our narrow-minded worship of laissez faire economic policy. That American sacred cow prevents us from using our government as an agency to promote both productivity and entrepreneurship in overseas trade as the Japanese and Germans so skillfully use theirs. Lawrence Cremin, probably the most capable historian of education our country has produced, had wise words to say on this topic, as on many others:

> American economic competitiveness with Japan and other nations is to a considerable degree a function of monetary, trade, and industrial policy, and of decisions made by the President and Congress, the Federal Reserve Board, and the federal Departments of the Treasury and Commerce and Labor. Therefore, to contend that problems of international competitiveness can be solved by education reform, especially education reform defined solely as school reform, is not merely utopian and millennialist, it is at best foolish and at worst a crass effort to direct attention away from those truly responsible for doing something about competitiveness and to lay the burden instead on the schools.[2]

I am not trying to argue against the prediction that future economic development in the United States will require more highly trained young men and women, although I find that prognosis haunted by at least two considerations. The first is the simple fact that the United States today has a higher proportion of its people attending and graduating from institutions of higher education than any other country in the world and is likely to continue in that favorable position. This is a remarkable achievement for a society as diverse as ours. But there is reason for concern about the availability of jobs for these well-prepared workers. On September 6, 1992, the *New York Times* carried an article on this aspect of the issue:

SAVING THE NATION WITH TESTS AND STANDARDS?

> The problem, it is turning out, is not so much the lack of education . . . The problem is a shortage of good jobs even for the educated . . . increasingly, the Labor Department reports, college graduates are taking lesser jobs—as sales clerks, for example—that don't require a college education. Indeed, on this Labor Day, it is worth pondering the paradox that companies in the forefront of the campaign for better public school education to solve the skills problem . . . have nevertheless shed skilled workers by the tens of thousands.[3]

This situation suggests to me that our most needed economic change may well be a job development program.

The second consideration that calls into question the importance to the economy of beefing up the learning levels of American workers is the very large number of jobs that keep even full-time workers in poverty or only slightly above it. This stern reality is reflected in the estimates of the availability of various types of jobs in the year 2000 (see Table 3). The categories of jobs with the highest rates of growth hold out a powerful promise for young people who are successful in school, but the jobs expected to be most plentiful as the next century begins are in low-paying categories that often lack benefits such as health insurance and that seldom offer opportunities for advancement. In all of the enthusiastic rhetoric about upgrading the workforce, no one ever explains how we will either upgrade these low-level service jobs or get rid of them.

In the meantime we continue to hold out to minority youth the glowing prospect of future careers if only they will work hard and succced in school. And yet we know that in reality many of them will either drop out or graduate and

Table 3
Employment opportunities in the year 2000

Fastest-growing jobs, 1988–2000

Job	Increase 1988–2000	Total jobs in 2000
Paralegal	75.3%	145,000
Medical assistant	70.0%	253,000
Radiologic technician	66.0%	218,000

Most plentiful jobs in the year 2000

Salesclerk	4,564,000
Janitor/maid	3,450,000
Waiter/waitress	2,337,000

Source: Harold Hodgkinson, *A Demographic Look at Tomorrow* (Washington, D.C.: Institute for Educational Leadership/Center for Demographic Policy, June 1992), p. 10. Data from U.S. Department of Labor, *Monthly Labor Review*, November 1989.

go into low-level jobs without a future. Racism enters into this situation. Too many white Americans instinctively see such jobs as the proper place for African Americans or Hispanics. The millennialism of the forecasts of good jobs for well-educated young workers will be a cruel hoax unless accompanied by increases in the minimum wage, universal coverage by health insurance, and genuine training opportunities with real continuity from training to employment. Today our country's safety net for youth has a big hole in it where each of these policies should be. President Bill Clinton has promised a direct attack on these problems which have been so long ignored, but at the time of this writing this attack remains more a hope than a reality.

More Tests, More Standards

These interrelated issues—the meaning of changes in average test scores, the reasons for America's slide in international competitiveness, and the prospects of young Americans for decent jobs—present both educators and political leaders with a complex task of diagnosis. We sense that something is awry with our country's children and youth. To return to my medical analogy, we seek to treat the patient's condition. The treatment we provide depends upon how we diagnose the illness.

I would argue that up to now the diagnosis has been superficial and simplistic. It has been centered on the belief that fixing the schools is the medicine that is needed, not recognizing that conditions in youngsters' lives outside of school are a major factor in their malaise. Furthermore, we have inaccurately diagnosed the shortcomings of schools. Asserting that schools were once good but have now turned bad, we have recommended a stronger dose of the old remedies of rigor and requirements rather than new prescriptions for making the classroom an exciting place, for enlisting families in schooling, for recognizing individual differences, and for adjusting the school to the student rather than the other way around.

As a result of this misdiagnosis, American educators now have before them a rapidly evolving plan for school improvement with two main characteristics: the offering of new American Achievement Tests for all levels of schooling, and a new set of standards in each major subject field. This program emerged from the Bush administration's publication in 1991 of *America 2000: An Education Strategy*, which I described in the Introduction.

Those who believe new tests and new standards will cure what ails American education should have paid more attention to recent history. Earlier attempts to use more tests to improve the quality of schools turned out to be a disaster for students, teachers, and schools. During the 1970s, amid growing concern about the quality of American schools (concern largely based on the misinterpretation of test scores), thirty-eight states launched mandatory testing programs to measure school performance or to define students' basic competency. The publication of *A Nation at Risk* in 1983 gave the testing bandwagon another push, and forty-seven states had newly legislated testing programs by the end of the decade. Negative effects of this massive increase in accountability and competency testing were reported from all over the country. Too much student time was devoted to testing that neither improved learning nor gave useful feedback to teachers or students. The tests used were machine-scored instruments unrelated to the curriculum of a classroom and reporting only comparative results rather than progress in what students were supposed to learn.

More important than this vacuum of learning created by the new volume of testing was the change in teaching practice it caused. School leadership reacted to the imposition of more standardized tests to assess schools by adapting classroom activities to fit the tests. Millions of children found themselves reading fewer stories, engaging in less discussion, and giving up group projects—all in favor of filling in the blanks on duplicated exercises resembling test questions.

In spite of a strong reaction against this kind of testing,

most of the tests that were legislated into the schools are still there. The reaction, however, has had some useful effects. It has helped to promote the move toward restructuring schools and the beginning of a realization that the key to creating a new and vibrant style of learning is to be found in fundamental change within classrooms. It has also sparked a growing interest in creating new forms of testing. Numerous efforts are under way to transform the tests used in schools into instruments that will stimulate students' interest in learning and that will show what parts of the curriculum students have adequately mastered and what parts need further attention. Tests intended to perform these functions are very different from those designed primarily to compare students' academic performance.

The American Achievement Tests referred to in *America 2000* are intended to embody new approaches to testing, and a number of agencies around the land are working hard to produce them and get them into use in the schools. The College Board is moving in that direction; the Educational Testing Service has been doing so for more than five years; and the so-called New Standards Project—a coalition of seventeen states, some school districts, the Learning Research and Development Center at the University of Pittsburgh, and the National Center on Education and the Economy in Rochester, New York—has moved, with support from major foundations, to plan ways both to develop new testing practices and to marry them to national standards. The National Council of Education Standards and Testing has recommended rapid implementation of the new tests and standards.

Changes in education usually come slowly; not surprisingly, these rather fast-moving developments are enmeshed in controversial discussions. Many testing experts have grave doubts about the possibility of developing tests that will provide useful information to students and teachers in classrooms and at the same time will offer a basis for awarding diplomas, selecting students for demanding academic programs in college, and assessing schools. There are deep concerns about the use of tests as the main leverage for bringing about changes in classrooms, and people who harbor these concerns point to the damage done in the recent past by just such a use of tests. Advocates of the new kinds of tests assert that they will avoid the damaging elements. Some educators believe the most promising approach lies not in imposing new national tests and standards but in training and retraining teachers and encouraging them to take part in their own reorienting of classroom practice—a viewpoint with which I substantially agree.

As for imposing common national standards on the diverse American population and its varied school systems, some see it as a much needed way to upgrade schooling by making sure that the tasks students undertake focus on significant subject matter and lead learners into more complex areas of thinking and understanding. They assert that national standards will avoid narrow requirements and set forth learning objectives in a broad and flexible framework. The state of California has recently adopted such an arrangement, and it calls it a "framework" rather than "standards," thereby implying more curricular flexibility for local schools and districts. Many others, in spite of such declarations, see national standards as a top-down system of control that will usurp the prerogatives of school districts, schools, and teachers—those who are aware of the widely varying educational needs and problems of local children and who need flexibility of both teaching strategies and subject matter to address them.

Many thoughtful educators are deeply concerned about the rush toward new tests and standards. A special issue of *Education Week* in 1992 published statements on this topic by a variety of educators and analysts of education; let me quote from a few of them.[4] Theodore R. Sizer, whose work with the Coalition of Successful Schools I praised in Chapter 6, has this to say:

> Who sets the standards and by what right? Who has the right to decide what U.S. history, in detail or in general, my child learns? Who has the right to decide how my kid is presented with questions of evolution? . . . [This question] deals with intellectual freedom, and it is a question that is very rarely discussed in the national debate over standards and assessments.

Deborah Meier, the New York City principal I also discussed approvingly in Chapter 6, does not mince words on this topic: "The pressure to look for answers via national curriculum and national testing is wrong headed, dangerous and counterproductive." And Gregory R. Anrig, president of the Educational Testing Service, which puts out the SAT and Advanced Placement exams for the College Board, is similarly direct: "There is a widely held concept that testing can drive instructional improvement and better learning. I believe that using accountability tests to drive educational reform is reckless driving. It won't work and it hasn't worked."

Donald R. Moore, executive director of Designs for Change in Chicago, who has been influential in bringing about the changes in the Chicago schools I mentioned in Chapter 8, seconds an important point I want to emphasize in this chapter:

> New approaches to student assessment will be constructive only if they are considered on an equal level with such hard issues as changing teachers' expectations for at risk students, principal accountability, tracking, teaching culturally diverse classrooms, parents' roles in school decision making and aiding their children's learning, support services for children, and suitable funding for schools.

Lauren Resnick and Marc Tucker, who head the New Standards Project, which is committed to developing the new standards that will supposedly cure what ails our schools, also express agreement with some important points I have been hammering at in this book. Here is Lauren Resnick, director of the Learning Research and Development Center at the University of Pittsburgh: "The New Standards Project is committed to the position that children will not be taking assessments unless their teachers have participated in the building and scoring of them." And Marc Tucker, president of the National Center on Education and the Economy: "Yes, we propose to abandon different standards for all. But we cannot do that without a commitment to provide a world in which every kid has a fair shot at achieving that standard."

A friend and colleague of mine at Harvard, Howard Gardner, puzzling over the wide spectrum of beliefs and feelings aroused by the proposals for national tests and standards, has identified two warring parties, the "hard heads" and the "soft hearts."[5] The hard heads, he explains, "insist that the time is at hand for a single set of national standards, possibly reflected in national curricula and syllabus and culminating in a high stakes test." The soft hearts, in contrast, "believe that any effective kind of education policy needs to be developed, almost from scratch, by stakeholders at the local level; soft hearts fear that educational reform will be doomed if we countenance a national or federal effort." Gardner sees himself as partly a soft heart because of his conviction that "no effort at reform can succeed unless it is understood and endorsed by teachers, parents, and others in the community." Then he shifts his allegiance to the hard heads because "it is not credible that every local county [I think he means school district] can come up with an effective education program for the twenty-first century. Local efforts need all the help they can get—and then some."

As a card-carrying "soft heart," I am willing to go along with this resolution of the controversy, and I will resist the temptation to accuse Howard Gardner of "carrying fire in one hand and water in the other." He's a very talented gentleman, and he can probably do it. His final paragraph presents a useful balance and might be the germ of a statement on which many educators could agree:

> Those who spurn any kind of national system fear politicization and inequity. These genuine fears can be met. Other countries have examination systems that are insulated from political pressure, and we can, if we wish, institute the same. Any system—including the present one—will have initial inequities. The important point is

that the system at least focus on the *right* kinds of performances and assessments, and that enough support be provided for all students and teachers so that the playing field is truly level. This can only come about if we have improved teacher education and sustained efforts to introduce the community to a new way of thinking about schooling.

I have two qualifications to make about Gardner's useful effort to bring peace and progress among education's leaders. First, almost all the "other countries" he refers to have less complex and less diverse societies than ours, a point that raises questions about how well their practices would work in the United States. Second, although I am one hundred percent in favor of his "level playing field," and although it echoes Marc Tucker's sentiments as quoted in *Education Week*, I seriously doubt that a level field will emerge from local, state, and federal actions, and I particularly doubt that it will emerge as rapidly as the bulldozer of new standards and new tests is proceeding. Will we hear from President Clinton about the plan for a level playing field? Will Secretary of Education, Richard Riley, push it with the same commitment that Secretary Alexander gave to tests and standards? Will the additional funds it will require be forthcoming from local and state taxes at a rate to keep up with the new funds for a vastly more expensive kind of testing? Who will educate the public about the requirement for a truly level field so they will support taxes to make it all possible? Will philanthropies like Pew and MacArthur, which are putting millions into new testing, step up to bat for a level playing field as they have for tests? What watchdog group removed from political pressures will take on the burden of publicizing the answers to questions like these, as the processes of building a totally new school system move forward? Creating a truly level playing field will not be an easy task, and it will cost billions.

An attribute of Howard Gardner's argument that I find particularly pleasing is that he sticks to education and doesn't drag in the economy to give urgency to the promotion of educational change. I believe it is important to move slowly in implementing such sweeping changes. Even good ideas for change may turn out to be damaging in practice if they are put into operation without the many other changes that should accompany them. Some of the antagonism to *America 2000* is a reaction to its hurry-up emphasis. The National Education Goals, if one takes them seriously, started with the naive assumption that their challenges could be met by the year 2000. Perhaps we weren't supposed to be literal minded about them but rather were to consider them a form of educational prayer that would give us something to reach for in the spirit of Browning's line, "A man's reach should exceed his grasp, or what's a heaven for?"

I hope that we can resolve these issues slowly—slowly enough to allow course corrections if we seem to be going astray; slowly enough to pursue various ways of leveling the playing field before we subject students to tests that will label them winners or losers; slowly enough to be sure teachers themselves have the opportunity to create the new classroom routines. If the relationship between our economy and the schools is as tenuous as I have argued it is, it provides no reason to rush into an effort for a quick fix that is unlikely to work. In addition, we need time to address other tasks than building new standards and new tests. New tests and new standards will not help teachers learn how to teach increasingly diverse groups of students, and putting new standards and tests into operation without adequate preparation of teachers to deal with them would be a major error. Teachers must have opportunities for practice with the new standards in the classroom before any children are forced to take tests that affect their futures. Giving unprepared youngsters tests in order to change schools is irresponsible. I have described it elsewhere as analogous to teaching swimming by throwing children into deep water: those who have pools at home will be most likely to survive.

Another factor to be considered in moving toward new standards and tests is the allocation of time in schools, which I discussed in Chapter 7. As new standards are introduced there will be many students who will need extra help. For some of these, additional time and additional services will be required, which in turn will require additional funding. Unless such needs are foreseen and dealt with, new tests and standards will reinforce the inequities we now have in our schools, and the educational gap between "haves" and "have nots" in America will continue to widen. The factory system of schooling fails because it doesn't adequately recognize that students learn at different rates and in different ways. Unless imaginative strategies to deal with those differences are developed for the new standards and tests, our schools will end up in a worse situation than they are in now. A hurried implementation of new tests and standards, without careful consideration of these issues, carries the strong possibility of repeating the sins we have already committed in the name of school reform.

Conclusion:
Thinking About Kids
and Education

It is high time for those of us who want to improve education to stop paying more attention to schools than to kids. We tend to think of children as if their lives could be divided up into neat compartments—school in one slot, home and community in another. We know that many children today come to school damaged by poverty, by disrupted family situations, by other factors that schools cannot influence, let alone control. We know, if we are willing to face it, that anything we can do to help families—by offering them paths out of poverty, for example—will be a real help to children. But we continue to define our task narrowly, as if the problems children and youth face can be solved by changing the schools.

It has become fashionable among education reformers to assume that the changes needed to help young Americans are academic in nature—more and better-taught mathematics, science, and other subjects. I do not mean to imply that academic objectives are unimportant, but I want to assert that a narrow strategy of promoting academic excellence will have disappointing effects. If we do not pay more attention to young people's social, physical, emotional, and moral development throughout early childhood and all the years of schooling, we may end up with adults who are wonderful computer operators and unbalanced human beings.

The answer of narrowly academic educators to this situation is simply that those elusive qualities of character and responsible behavior are mostly the business of the family. And they are right! But the family is no longer there in the same sense that it was in simpler times. Our high divorce rate may free adults from frustrating circumstances, but it damages children; single-parent families are less able to provide the emotional support kids need. The growing pervasiveness of poverty magnifies the damage from the neglect of children, but that damage occurs at all economic levels.

Americans are wary about letting the long arm of government reach into the private affairs of the family. Numerous other countries have long had social support programs that our children are denied. Back in the early 1970s we almost had legislation to provide child care services—but President Nixon vetoed it on the grounds that American tradition was for families to look after their own children. Twenty years later we are still without adequate day care in this country; thousands of children come home from school each day to households without adults present. Many more children are handicapped by poor nutrition, lack of health care, and other side effects of poverty and family disruption. Schools find themselves struggling to teach math and history to students whose lives beyond the schoolhouse door provide limited support for learning, and too much anxiety.

Paying for Prevention

We need to change our focus from trying to patch up children after they are already damaged to aiding families to prevent the damage in the first place. A preventive approach to such ills will not come into being unless we can somehow rally major political support in our country for significant action on the needs of children and youth. This action must include both providing adequate and equitable funding for schools and improving the living standards of poor families to give their children a better chance for success. Clearly if we are to take such action we will have to find a great deal of money somewhere.

One way to come up with the money would be to reduce the many supports we now grant to middle-class families through social programs and our federal tax system—such as tax deductions for mortgage interest and subsidized education at state colleges and universities—in order to make a transfer of tax dollars to the poor. Looking at past responses to programs based on need, however, I have to say experience tells us that most Americans don't want to be generous toward the poor.

Perhaps we would be more willing to do what European countries do with programs for children and what we now do in our Social Security system for older people: to give *all* families the right to child support, health insurance coverage, and other social necessities. By offering child subsidies to *all* families, we just might bring it off—particularly if we changed our tax system to include a value-added tax instead of insisting on new progressive income tax levies. Getting broad-based political support from America's middle class to help the poor and only the poor has about as much chance as the proverbial snowball in hell. But the Social Security system is widely supported politically because it protects not only the poor but everyone in the country who works and families of workers as well. Maybe by designing a social program for all families we can manage to help those who really need it.[1]

The other half of the money question is how to fund the schools fairly so that children's educational opportunities are not decided by the property taxes their communities are willing to vote for. As I argued in Chapter 5, the way we pay for our schools is unfair to many of the students in them; it is not well adapted to current thinking about giving schools more discretion in managing their own affairs; and it is encrusted with multiple bureaucracies that not only cost money but also inhibit useful educational change. There has been some interest in finding improved systems of fiscal planning; a bill in the Senate Committee on Labor and Human Resources in the fall of 1992 would have set up a major study of the way schools are financed. It sought a large-scale, nonpartisan effort to seek a more rational and more equitable system of paying for schools with local, state, and national funds. There was no action on this legislation, but the concept is still alive in the Senate committee and there is some interest in it in the House of Representatives. My guess is that both houses of Congress might get behind this proposal if the President would give it a push. Tampering with the basic funding of schools has major political hazards for members of Congress, and White House support would ease the pressure.

Goals of Education

As must be clear by now, I am not satisfied with the National Education Goals set out by the governors and George Bush in 1989. Those six goals say nothing about making our increasingly diverse society function better and more fairly. They largely ignore the family and the community as educational institutions. They carry no commitment to our teaching force in return for the mammoth changes they ask its members to make. And they do not address the fact that many American students attend schools that are starved for funding.

Now that we have elected a new President, it is a good time to reconsider these inadequate goals. I propose adding four new goals to the list.[2]

One of the four I have already stated in Chapter 8, quoting George Madaus: "By the year 2000 America will have the best prepared, most highly respected teaching force in the world." The federal government could well fashion some new legislation to support progress in this realm. In the late 1960s, the Congress passed the Education Professions Development Act, which created a broad federal mission to encourage improvements in teacher preparation, the in-service renewal of teachers' skills, and the preparation of principals and superintendents. But this legislation was abandoned during the Nixon years, and few of today's educators have ever heard of it. Both the salaries and the social status of teachers in the United States are far lower than those of teachers in the countries with which we compete. Even the Bush administration took a shot at this problem in *America 2000* by suggesting lots of prizes for successful teachers. If President Bush had carried out that plan, he would have worn out the Rose Garden but done very little for the teaching profession.

A second new goal would call for a totally new plan for financing public schools in the United States, to be launched by the year 2000. The plan should be based on the needs of children and youth so that the accident of where a student lives will no longer determine the quality of schooling that student can receive. State, local, and federal roles in financing schools will all have to be rethought if we are to reach this goal, as will equity for both students and taxpayers. As noted earlier, there is genuine interest in Congress in attacking this problem.

My third new goal would be to have all schools include in their vision statements a commitment to broaden students' understanding of the diversity of groups that make up American society. Students in American schools must learn about one another, not just by celebrating unfamiliar holidays and other superficial activities, but by seriously studying other cultures, traditions, and historical experiences. Future generations must know how to deal with diversity in positive ways if our society is to avoid being split into hostile factions. President Bill Clinton has done a classy job of expressing a general position on this topic, and of practicing what he preaches in appointing his cabinet. Leaders in schools should accept his challenge and match his actions.

Finally, and perhaps most important, we need an educational goal recognizing that the family is an educational institution and that schools alone cannot provide all the stimulation and guidance young people need. The first of the original six goals does touch on this issue: "All children will start school ready to learn." But it is cut off at the knees by the implication that family support is needed only to get started. Family and community supports are needed throughout the years of schooling and beyond. That first goal should be changed to carry the full message of parental obligation through childhood and adolescence, and of public commitment to support and educate families needing help with this responsibility.

Implementing this fourth new goal will require a major shift in public attitudes toward aid to poor families. The twentieth century has precedents for such fundamental change: the growth of democracy with the popular election of senators, and suffrage for women, before and just after World War I; the launching of the Social Security system in the 1930s; the advances in civil rights and human services in the Johnson years. These changes did not come easily. In the 1930s, for example, some Americans railed against the Social Security program as a socialistic departure from American principles. And yet today it is one of the most popular and politically secure government programs we have. What is necessary to accomplish such change is a commitment by political leadership at the highest level. If the President now in the White House will push to move our country forward on behalf of children and families as he is already pushing for the reform of health care, the last years of this century may well bring constructive social change worthy to be mentioned with those earlier achievements. The realization that education is a much broader concept than schooling makes it clear that our country's educational goals have an important place on the agenda of social change.

Lawrence Cremin, shortly before he died, penned some wise words pointing out the more comprehensive and fundamental goal of education. I close this book with his statement in the hope that it will be heeded by all of us who are thinking about kids and about their schools:

> [T]he aim of education is not merely to make parents, or citizens, or workers, or indeed to surpass the Russians or the Japanese, but ultimately to make human beings who will live life to the fullest, who will continually add to the quality and the meaning of their experience and to their ability to direct that experience, and who will participate actively with their fellow human beings in the building of a good society.[3]

NOTES

Chapter 1. Misuse of Tests to Measure Schools

1. *A Nation at Risk: The Imperative for Educational Reform* (Washington, D.C.: National Commission on Excellence in Education, 1983), pp. 8–9.
2. Clark Kerr, "Is Education Really All That Guilty?" *Education Week*, February 27, 1991, p. 30.
3. Willard Wirtz et al., *On Further Examination: Report of the Advisory Panel on the Scholastic Aptitude Test Score Decline* (New York: College Examination Board, 1977).
4. Harold Howe II, "Let's Have Another SAT Score Decline," *Phi Delta Kappan*, November 1991, pp. 192–203.
5. George Madaus, personal communication, September 1992.
6. Wirtz et al., *On Further Examination*, p. 42.
7. Two articles in the *Phi Delta Kappan*, October 1992, present strong analyses of this subject: Gerald W. Bracey, "The Second Report on the Condition of Public Education," pp. 104–117; and Richard M. Jeager, "World Class Standards, Choices, and Privatization: Weak Measurement Serving Presumptive Policy," pp. 118–128.
8. *A Nation at Risk*, p. 8.
9. I am indebted to Iris Rotberg for the main substance of the discussion that follows. See Iris C. Rotberg, "I Never

Promised You First Place," *Phi Delta Kappan*, December 1990, pp. 296–303.

10. Ibid., p. 299.
11. Ibid., p. 303.
12. Quoted in Ian Westberg, "Comparing American and Japanese Achievement: Is the United States Really a Low Achiever?" *Educational Researcher,* June/July 1992, p. 18.

Chapter 2. Families, Communities, and Children

1. Educational Testing Service, *America's Smallest School: The Family* (Princeton, N.J.: ETS Policy Information Center, 1992), p. 4.
2. Emory Bundy quoted in *The Forgotten Half: Final Report of the William T. Grant Foundation Commission on Work, Family, and Citizenship* (Washington, D.C., 1988), p. 63.
3. James S. Coleman, "Families and Schools," *Educational Researcher*, August–September 1987, pp. 36–37.
4. *The Forgotten Half*, pp. 61–62.
5. Educational Testing Service, *America's Smallest School*, p. 38.
6. Children's Defense Fund, *Vanishing Dreams: The Economic Plight of America's Young Families* (1992), as reported in *Education Week*, April 22, 1992.
7. Sanford M. Dornbusch and Kenneth D. Wood, "Family Processes and Educational Achievement," in *Education and the American Family*, ed. William J. Weston (New York: New York University Press, 1989), pp. 66–91.
8. Urban Institute data given in Children's Defense Fund, *Child Poverty in America* (Washington, D.C., 1991), p. 26.
9. Robinson G. Hollister, Jr., *New Evidence about Effective Training Strategies* (New York: Rockefeller Foundation, 1990).
10. 167 Holland Street, Somerville, Mass. 02144.

11. Children's Defense Fund, *Child Poverty in America*.
12. *Facing the Challenge: The Report of the Twentieth Century Fund Task Force on School Governance* (New York: Twentieth Century Fund, 1992).
13. Marion W. Pines, *Family Investment Strategies: Improving the Lives of Children and Communities* (Partners for Livable Places, 1429 21st Street, Washington, D.C. 20036, 1992), p. 30.
14. *ERIC Review* 2, no. 1, 1992.
15. Children's Defense Fund, *Child Poverty in America*, p. 27.
16. Gunnar Myrdal, *An American Dilemma: The Negro Problem and Modern Democracy* (New York and London: Harper and Brothers, 1944), vol. 1, p. xliii.
17. Lisbeth B. Schorr, "Successful Early Interventions Aimed at Reducing Intergenerational Disadvantage," paper presented at Harvard University Seminar on Poverty, April 4, 1988; based on Lisbeth B. Schorr with Daniel Schorr, *Within Our Reach: Breaking the Cycle of Disadvantage* (New York: Anchor Press/Doubleday, 1988).

Chapter 3. Race, Culture, and Education

1. Quotes taken from Gary Orfield, *The Reconstruction of Southern Education* (New York: John Wiley and Sons, 1969), pp. 294–296.
2. Andrew Hacker, *Two Nations* (New York: Charles Scribner's Sons, 1992), p. 219.
3. Arthur Schlesinger, *The Disuniting of America* (New York: Norton, 1992), p. 14.
4. Gary Orfield and Franklin Monfort with the assistance of Anita Stoll and Rafael Heller, *Status of School Desegregation: The Next Generation*, Report to the National School Boards Association (Cambridge, Mass.: Metropolitan Opportunity Project, Harvard University, March 1992), p. 36.

5. Henry Louis Gates, Jr., *Loose Canons: Notes on the Culture Wars* (New York: Oxford University Press, 1992), p. xv.
6. David S. Tatel, "Desegregation vs. School Reform," *Stanford Law and Policy Review*, Winter 1992–93, p. 61.
7. Ibid., p. 66.
8. Schlesinger, *The Disuniting of America*, pp. 137–138.
9. Henry Louis Gates, Jr., *Rethinking Schools* (Milwaukee), October/November 1991, p. 1.

Chapter 4. Choice: The Millennium?

1. John E. Chubb and Terry M. Moe, *Politics, Markets, and America's Schools* (Washington, D.C.: Brookings Institution, 1990).
2. Editorial, *Boston Globe*, February 13, 1991.
3. Owen B. Butler, "Some Doubts on School Vouchers," *New York Times*, July 5, 1991, p. A–21.
4. See Richard Fossey, "School Choice Legislation: A Survey of the States," Center for Policy Research on Education, Harvard Graduate School of Education, September 1991.

Chapter 5. Does Money Make a Difference?

1. *The Forgotten Half: Final Report of the William T. Grant Foundation Commission on Work, Family, and Citizenship* (Washington, D.C., 1988).
2. Editorial, *New York Times*, November 29, 1992.
3. U.S Department of Education, National Center for Education Statistics, *The Condition of Education, 1992* (Washington, D.C.), table 48–2.
4. Mr. Justice Marshall Dissenting, *San Antonio School District v. Rodriguez* 411 U.S. 1 (1973).
5. David C. Berliner, "Education Reform in an Era of Disinformation," paper presented at a meeting of the

American Association of Colleges for Teacher Education, San Antonio, Texas, February 1992.

6. Fred Branfman, "Passing On Our Troubles," *Boston Globe*, July 26, 1992, p. 63.

Chapter 6. Students Are People!

1. Richard J. Light, *Explorations with Students and Faculty about Teaching, Learning, and Student Life*, Harvard Assessment Seminars, 2nd report (Cambridge, Mass.: Harvard University, 1992).

2. This oversimplified statement about Ted Sizer's thinking can be filled in by reading his two books about a fictitious high school teacher called Horace, a person whose speculations provide some of the best food for educational thought in the current reform movement: *Horace's Compromise: The Dilemma of the American High School* (Boston: Houghton Mifflin, 1984), and *Horace's School: Redesigning the American High School* (Boston, Houghton Mifflin, 1992).

3. John Goodlad, *A Place Called School* (New York: McGraw Hill, 1983).

4. Wendy S. Hopfenberg, Henry M. Levin, Gail Meister, and John Rogers, "Accelerated Schools," paper prepared at the Stanford University School of Education, August 1990, p. 8.

5. Deborah Meier, quoted in the *New York Times*, August 10, 1992, p. B3.

6. Joan Lipsitz, *Growing Up Forgotten: A Review of Research and Programs Concerning Early Adolescence*, report to the Ford Foundation (Lexington, Mass.: Lexington Books, 1977).

7. *Turning Points: States in Action* (Washington, D.C.: Council of Chief State School Officers, Resource Center on Educational Equity, 1992).

Chapter 7. Time: The Procrustean Bed

1. Ernest Boyer, *High School* (New York: Harper and Row, 1983), p. 60.
2. I first heard this in the late 1950s when it was presented by the admissions officer of the U.S. Military Academy at West Point during a College Board meeting.
3. *They Went to College Early,* Fund for the Advancement of Education, Evaluation Report no. 2 (New York, 1957), pp. 5–10.
4. The *Harvard Education Letter*, September/October 1992, provides a useful overview of the literature on tracking. The work of Jeannie Oakes has been particularly influential; see, for example, Jeannie Oakes, *Educational Matchmaking: Academic and Vocational Tracking in Comprehensive High Schools* (Santa Monica, Calif.: Rand, 1992).
5. Joseph M. Carroll, *The Copernican Plan: Restructuring the American High School* (Andover, Mass.: Regional Laboratory for Educational Improvement of the Northeast and Islands, 1989).

Chapter 8. Classrooms, Teachers, and Principals

1. Edward Pauly, *The Classroom Crucible* (New York: Basic Books, 1991), p. 2.
2. Deborah Meier, "Reinventing Teaching," *Teachers College Record* 93, no. 4 (Summer 1992): 606–607.
3. *Barriers to Excellence: Our Children at Risk* (Boston: National Coalition of Advocates for Students, 1985).
4. Susan Moore Johnson, *Teachers at Work* (New York: Basic Books, 1990), p. 338.
5. Meier, "Reinventing Teaching," pp. 596, 601.
6. Pauly, *Classroom Crucible*, p. 16.

7. Johnson, *Teachers at Work*, p. 118.

8. Adria Steinberg and Anne Wheelock, "After Tracking— What? Middle Schools Find New Answers," *Harvard Education Letter*, September/October 1992, p. 1.

9. A good way to sample Wigginton's work and that of the students is to read *I Wish I Could Give My Son a Wild Raccoon*, edited and with an introduction by Eliot Wigginton (Garden City, N.Y.: Anchor Books/Doubleday, 1976).

10. Kim Marshall, "Teachers and Schools: What Makes a Difference," manuscript, 1992, p. 11. (A later version of this paper appeared in *Daedalus*, Winter 1993, pp. 209–242.)

11. Ibid., p. 19.

12. Thomas James, "Interim Report from a State-Level Study of the Michigan Partnership for Education," manuscript, October 1992, pp. 1–2.

13. John W. Gardner, *Self Renewal: The Individual and the Innovative Society* (New York: Harper and Row, 1963), p. xvi.

14. George Madaus, "A National Testing System: Manna from Above," manuscript, Center for the Study of Testing, Evaluation and Educational Policy, Boston College, 1992.

15. Richard Murnane et al., *Who Will Teach? Policies That Matter* (Cambridge, Mass.: Harvard University Press, 1991), pp. 14–15.

16. Marshall, "Teachers and Schools," p. 19.

Chapter 9. Saving the Nation with Tests and Standards?

1. Most of the following items come from David C. Berliner, "Education Reform in an Era of Disinformation," paper presented at a meeting of the American Association of Colleges for Teacher Education, San Antonio, Texas, February 1992.

2. Lawrence Cremin, *Popular Education and Its Discontents* (New York: Harper and Row, 1990), p. 103.
3. Louis Uchitelle, "America Isn't Creating Enough Jobs, and No One Seems to Know Why," *New York Times*, September 6, 1992, p. 4–1.
4. I have room here only for excerpts from what they had to say; for the full statements, see *Education Week: Special Report*, June 17, 1992.
5. Howard Gardner, "Combining Two Cornerstones," *Education Week: Special Report*, June 17, 1992.

Conclusion: Thinking About Kids and Education

1. This argument emerged from conversations with Harold Wilensky of the University of California at Berkeley.
2. This listing of new goals tracks an article of mine entitled "We Need Four More Education Goals," which appeared in *Education Week*, February 3, 1993. I recapitulate it here with permission from *Education Week*.
3. Lawrence A. Cremin, *Popular Education and Its Discontents* (New York: Harper and Row, 1990), p. 125.

INDEX